Cosmic DNA

The Joy of Astrology Inference

Kim Frantzve

Cosmic DNA
The Joy of Astrology Inference

ISBN-13: 978-0-9894174-0-2

Published by
MindSpa Press
5547 South Kimbark Avenue, #1
Chicago, Illinois 60637 USA

Illustrations by Mary Lindsay
Edited by Kimberly Norton Matthews
Design and layout by Lighthouse24

Dedication—

To Jasmine Joy,
you were my motivation
to complete this book.
You are a gifted and insightful
astrological protégé of your father.

Table of Contents

Introduction

Our biological DNA has a genetic, molecular encoding comprised of a sequence of bases. We all have the same DNA components, but it is the sequence of DNA bases that influences our unique characteristics. Our Cosmic DNA operates in a similar fashion. We are a microcosm of the solar system energies, and it is the sequence of these energies that gives us our unique traits. As a professional astrologer, the goal is to decode the Cosmic DNA represented in the astrological chart in order to infer the solar genetics of our clients.

In a dynamic Astrology model, energy is active, interactive and just like physics, it relates to forces that produce motion. Each person represents a series of dynamics that have intersected at the moment of birth. When you look at energy it is not static, it is relational. It is emitting certain frequencies and attracting frequencies. By understanding dynamic prototypes and principles, you can interpret energy, and see how the combinations of energy operate as alchemy because it is the interface of these dynamics that often creates reality.

Dynamics between people are combinations. If you are dynamically emitting an energy that is self stabilized, you will attract energy that seeks to be stabilized, and you will find yourself to be playing that role to others. If you have an abundance of energy that needs to receive from others, you will repeatedly place yourself in situations that force others to give to you, or you will be interfacing with people who require your assistance. If you innately give to others, then there will be a whole slew of opportunities presented that seek to receive from your innate giving energy.

Astrology consists of so many complex mathematical, philosophical, and metaphysical schools of thought. This book does not provide all the fundamental astrological principles. It is an overview of energetic components and interpretive tools for those who already know astrology and those who seek to understand people's charts in a more dynamic, real-time way.

Chapter One
Our Solar Map

Each of us has a story reflected within the solar system. As we journey through life, we may strive to discipline the body, elevate the mind and evolve our spirit. By understanding the energetic components of our story, and how they interact dynamically inside and outside of us, we can extract the information and knowledge that contains our actions, behaviors and motivations. Within this realization, we can begin to understand what makes some areas of our lives more challenging than others.

All of us come into the world with a unique Cosmic DNA. This cosmic map defines how we see reality on multiple levels, from the organic, physical self to the evolved social and spiritual self. The basic astrological wheel is a symbolic and philosophical representation of our personal evolution, our past life, the situation we were born into, and experiential dynamics in this lifetime.

Your chart will indicate the journey you are on and the different struggles or areas of focus that will consume you in this lifetime. Some people may be in repeated patterns, unable to have any completion and satisfaction in certain areas of life. The chart also shows where one may be highly evolved, thus attracting people that need to be rescued, educated or served.

Your personal inventory is a composite of energies operating on the mental, physical, social and spiritual realms. Each component has a different degree of proficiency and maturity, as well as conscious or subconscious input into various areas of life. Some energies are elevated in spiritual understanding, often superseding our human consciousness. When this happens, we may be playing roles to others without knowing the reason.

Our COSMIC DNA is Revealed in our Astrological Chart

In an attempt to understand our approach to the world around us, we must first understand the various genetic codes and cosmic codes that we are responding to as human beings. From an energetic perspective, these become our cosmic blueprint. Our natal chart is an energetic profile based on our birth date, birth time and place of birth.

By understanding our Cosmic DNA, we can understand what we are energetically attracted to in life, and what is drawn to us. This knowledge can help us become more aware of our different personalities, especially the ones that have become splintered into separate realities, separate relationships, and different degrees of completion.

The signs that the planets were in at birth reflect the planetary configuration when you were born. This is the activity in the inner part of the chart. It represents the energetic components the soul will carry to express itself. The signs ruling the houses, or the outer ring of the chart, are contingent on your time of birth and represent the experiences you will encounter. The outer part of the chart represents the conditions you are here to work through and the inside planets show how you will deal with the conditions.

The chart shows who we are as physical, social and spiritual beings. The lower half of the chart (houses 1-6) represents our organic being, our physical development and evolvement. It is our perceived sense of self, and the body, or vehicle, by which we are operating. The upper half of the chart (houses 7-12) represents our social and spiritual development and evolvement. It is the world where we dissolve our individuality to become responsible, committed and devoted. With each progressive energy field, the physical body's perceptions become less of a component and determinant of what constitutes maturity and love.

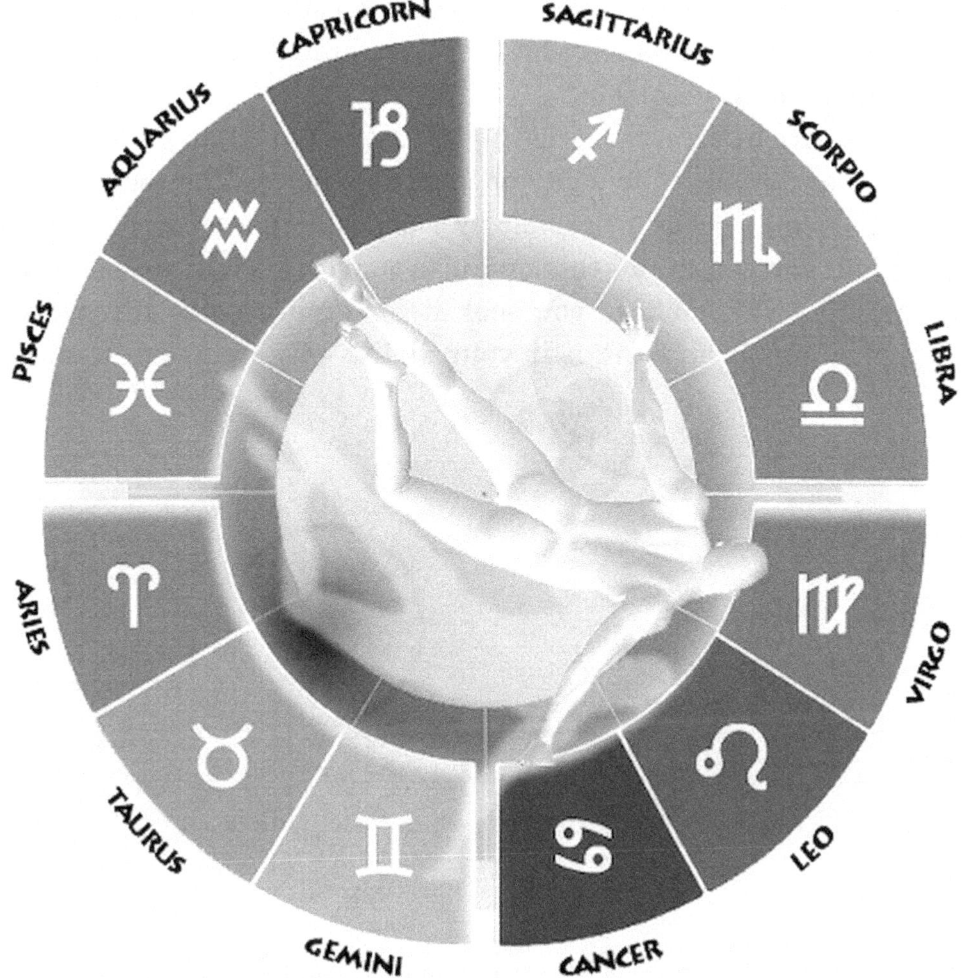

The wheel is comprised of 360 degrees and divided into four quadrants. Each quadrant is divided into thirds (called houses), which represent various principles and relationship models. Each house has 30 degrees and the first house starts on the left side of the equator (9:00 PM). There are twelve houses ruled by the signs: Aries, Taurus, Gemini, Cancer, Leo, Virgo, Libra, Scorpio, Sagittarius, Capricorn, Aquarius and Pisces.

When you look at interpreting the astrological chart, it represents fields of knowledge, behavior and experiences within your personal and social arenas of life. It demonstrates whether you use your encounters or feelings as reality. Or, do you use philosophies, responsibilities, mental constructs or creativity to define yourself?

The signs (Aries - Pisces) represent developmental stages and regions of knowledge that contain, represent and dispense energy. They become archetypes, possessing certain principles, characteristics and symbolic, philosophical representations that organize our story. What you want shows up in your PLANET. Where you seek it, or area of your life, is in the HOUSE. How you go about it, is in your SIGN.

Chapter Two

Solar Bodies

Since the Sun is a star, the Moon is a satellite of Earth, and Pluto demoted to a "dwarf-planet," this chapter heading "Solar Bodies" is my term for what traditional astrology authors refer to as "Planets." The solar system progresses from dense matter (the inner planetary world of Mercury, Venus, Earth, and Mars) to broken down matter (the asteroid belt) to gases (the outer planetary world: Jupiter, Saturn, Uranus, Neptune, and Pluto).

Each planet represents a principle that functions to impact, organize, contain and define reality. It has an influence in terms of how we see ourselves, how we define ourselves and how we see the world around us, as well as how the world is presenting, defining and organizing itself. Planetary energies operate simultaneously and continuously, to a lesser or greater degree. When a planet is "discovered" by us, its energy literally manifests on Earth in tangible forms.

The solar system is not static; it is in constant motion. As the planets move forward, their movement is counter-clockwise in the chart, influencing different areas of our lives. There may be personal periods of acceleration, transition or change in the ways we interact and relate to the world, people and situations in life. It also influences these same transitions socially. Astrologers refer to this as transits. I am not presenting information on transits in this book; however, all serious astrologers study the cycles of planets, and transits are part of most astrological sessions because they reflect what is happening to clients in real time. Once you understand your Cosmic DNA you are in a position to explore what transits will be applicable.

The Solar System Has Three Major Regions.

There are the inner planets (Mercury, Venus, Earth and Mars), the asteroid belt (thousands of fragmented planets) and the outer planets (Jupiter, Saturn, Uranus, Neptune and Pluto). Each of these regions become solar dimensions and represent a different phase of how we see ourselves and seek security, who we use to source and supply our needs, what is required to maintain a relationship to our source, and how this process regenerates itself.

The inner planets, (Mercury, Venus, Earth and Mars) are closest to the Sun, and represent our biological system, our human development and the relationship with our mother, our father and family. First I feel, I perceive, I experience, I interact and finally I create. The Sun and Mercury is one's feelings. The Venetian phase is perceptive – I perceive something, which creates my personal myths. The third phase is Earth, where we begin to overcome gravity and can stand on our own and interact. The fourth phase is Mars, where we act and join with another person. Mars is action, sexuality and procreation.

The inner planetary process is the 3D world. It uses the body and feelings to interpret reality. One's thoughts originate from perceptions, judgments, conclusions and whatever impacts us in the moment.

The inner planetary perception:

- Uses the 5 senses to process experiences,
- Feelings and emotions dictate perception
- Operates by physical awareness
- Conclusion and opinion based
- Lives in light and dark, cold and warmth

The inner planets represent the evolution of the human form, and the replicated actions and behaviors to meet our necessity as physical creatures. This includes desires, emotions, perceptions, connections, and the human interactions, which create our perception of reality and truth. The basic principle of mammals is protection of the young by an individual or group who stand between the random universe and the young's security. The young learn to trust the interactions with their own kind and bonding is this glue of security.

The inner planetary bonding world continuously adjusts and maintains an emotional, physical, and psychological bubble around the young so they can mature to become an active member and participant in the group. The bonding world's foundation builds around the consistency and warmth of the Sun, source, or Mother. This develops into a psychological world of trust.

The foundation of how our biological/physical self processes information is through an internal system of feelings and emotions (pain, pleasure, happiness, sadness, misery, depression, anger), sensory interpretations (hear, see, smell, taste, and touch) memory retention, obsessions and compulsions, and connections and separations. This is a "world of trust," which governs our life and death, bonding and procreation. It revolves around self, family, interpersonal relationships, mothers, fathers, children, tribes, and clans. It constitutes connectedness and the group's relationship to their environment.

The **asteroid belt** is thousands of dwarf planets and particles. The asteroid belt is "the void," an area in space where particles are fragmented and discombobulated.

The **outer planets** (Jupiter, Saturn, Uranus, Neptune and Pluto), which are further away from the Sun, will not have the same heat. They come from the same components of the Sun, but do not get the radiation of the Sun itself, because they are too far. They can only influence life they cannot create life. The discovery of the outer planets—Jupiter, Saturn, Uranus, Neptune, and Pluto—brought in a new perception of reality that was idea-based.

As you stand on the Earth and look up to the sky, you can see the Sun, Mercury, Venus, Mars, Jupiter and Saturn. With these planets, you are in relationship to what you can see. These planets organize and energetically influence the physical realm of reality. Once you start going further out in space you are influenced by things you cannot see, but they are still part of the solar system. They are still part of you. The outer planets are so far away from the Sun that that their temperatures are incomprehensibly cold and the atmosphere is all whirling gas. These planets have an order as well, and they represent our societal order.

There is a difference in the solar system between the seen and unseen influences that take place in the world; the planets seen with the naked eye and the planets discovered through technology. The influence from the unseen world will bring forms to the planet (inventions and devices) that were not known or seen prior to the discovery of that planet, and it will shift the very nature of how we operate in the physical body. Each planet and their different orbs, or paths they take around the Sun, appear to represent fields of knowledge.

When we are born, we are influenced by more than just the warmth of our mother's body, the relationship with our father and family, our hereditary genes, physical body and immediate environment, which are all inner planetary influences. The outer planets also influence us. Jupiter, or knowledge, defines and redefines reality by how the societal order stipulates the roles of males and females and defines the value, conditioning and usage of children.

We cannot escape Saturn's role in organizing and structuring boundaries and laws, which forces our body, as well as society to align to rules and regulations. Or, how everyone interfaces with Uranus energy, the manifestation of new ideas, inventions, technology, devices and things we add to ourselves such as bottles and formula, or television and computers. There is also Neptune's influence, which is the recreation and projection of reality, and the ability to remote view through images projected to us through microscopes, telescopes, television, movies and advertising. Since 1930, we have added the influence of Pluto, the last known solar body at the end of our solar system. It represents the death of one way of being, and then transformation, regeneration and rebirth.

The energy of the inner planets formulates who we are as physical creatures and dominates our early childhood, family life and approach to relationships. The energy of the outer planets influences us psychologically, socially and symbolically. Understanding the outer planets will give you insight into how you have integrated those energies into your personality.

Jupiter

Jupiter is the first planet of the outer planetary world and the largest planet in our solar system. Called the second Sun, not only because of its size but also because of its influence, it is the planet of philosophy, religion, and ideas, which interprets and defines reality. Jupiter creates the philosophical world and converts organic beings to reorganize their actions, behaviors, and perceptions. It converts humans and animals into psychological species, which is the first step in preparing human beings and animals for collective usage.

There are processes and disciplines created that encourage and train us to be obedient and disciplined to particular ideas. This conditioned compliance surpasses what we may subjectively think or emotionally feel and brings forth promises to increase our probability of having consistent and beneficial experiences in our life. Jupiter not only defines what we are experiencing, but also serves to increase the probability of a safe, explainable, and rational universe. This contains and organizes our perceptions within some universal definition.

Jupiter represents the first influence to reorganize the organic model and its diversified perceptions into some universal definition. It represents religious ideologies and universal principles about how life should be defined, contained, and organized. It is how we consciously define what reality is, and then in combination with Saturn, how society uses this disciplined version of us.

Saturn

Before Saturn was discovered you could not ask how far it was from someone's house to yours. There was no mutually agreed way to measure anything. Saturn's influence measures and defines time and space and we can now answer: "What is this, how far is this, and how long will this take?"

If Saturn gets a hold of anything, it keeps reducing it until it gets to a finite definition. From a big space, it takes it to the smallest denominator possible. It measures everything. Saturn's purpose is to dispense information without gaps, reducing misunderstanding to bring a uniform way to interpret something. Saturn divides space into separate compartments or grids and the grids keep energy divided.

Saturn is ownership of land and boundaries. We have nations, countries, states, cities, and towns, all in distinct boundaries. It takes a day and compartmentalizes it into hours, minutes, seconds. Saturn's job is linking things by ownership of land until we define, mark and own every inch of the world. Saturn restricts reality and places defined controls on people with laws, rules, and order. It then solidifies this as reality by a system of punishment if our behavior does not align. It grounds an idea to the body, so it becomes a physical law, and conditions how the body will perceive reality. Our whole system of 30 day billing cycles is a Saturn process overlaid on us.

Saturn and Jupiter combined is the world of letters and numbers.

The system of letters and numbers form science, allowing us to organize and define all things. It defines everything that can be seen even the subatomic world. It also tends to organize people by beliefs and laws. It will institutionalize you; put you in school, corporations, church, and even jail. Ideas are redefining reality more than our human interactions, training and transforming the physical body into utilization by influences governed by thought.

In 1781, Uranus was discovered. This is an important milestone for humankind because it was the birth of Artificial Life on the planet. It created acceleration of the mechanically driven world and the movement of devices interfacing with human beings on a mass level, dramatically altering how we interface as organic beings on the planet. The information organizing our current societal structure and our cultural psychology is that of Artificial Intelligence. This Uranus influence is growing and will eventually produce more matter than currently exists on the planet.

The creation of artificial life operates by combining energy dynamically to create new objects not seen before. Uranus takes existing form and recreates the relationship between things to create new matter. In its acceleration, it will eventually produce as much, if not more, artificial matter, than biological life. As humans, we may one day be an endangered species replaced by Artificial Intelligence as the new life form on Earth.

The Jupiter world uses humans because it converts people to represent its beliefs. Saturn uses people through obligation and duty to be a component to its worlds, but Uranus could not use humans to accelerate at its rate of speed because the human form is too slow, and it interjects too much subjectivity. Human beings as a knowledge-gathering device are too inadequate to dispense information on a continuous basis. Our energy cannot go 24/7, cannot process without going through some organic perceptions, and will continue to misread reality because we construct, define, and organize reality from the physical body's perspective.

Since the discovery of Uranus we have been a device driven, technological society operating from the outer planetary spheres of devices and projection, spacecrafts, TV, movies, satellites, radar, sound devices, scanning devices, computers etc. Currently, our experiences are more from this world than they are from the human based world. We are not in a primate reality based on touch, taste, and smell. We operate more from the body's detached tools of sight and sound. This world is replicating exponentially, as generations of technology become obsolete, sometimes within months.

With Neptune's detection in 1846, photography showed up and ushered in the world of projection. Our lives were never going to be the same again. This new influence projects reality to us, conveying experiences our physical body cannot verify. With Neptunian energy, we are no longer limited to what the five senses can see, perceive, or verify. We now have images projected to us that influence and motivate us. The world of photography, cinematography, television, advertising and all forms of mass media exist via the world of projection, and they selectively project images and create views that we do not physically verify, but believe them to be true anyway. Millions of people are directed and swayed by the images and messages projected unto them through mass media.

Psychology is Neptune generated. In the last 100 years, Neptune brought psychology to the forefront. The whole psychological field is human's projecting back to themselves. Projections are models of behavior considered "normal" and "abnormal." The whole concept of "disorders" is based on a projection of what should be, and defines behavior outside of that as psychological illness. Neptune brings the science of mind and the beginning of new thought religions. With Neptune's influence, human beings now lived in a mechanical world in which they could generate their own thoughts and become their own creators. Before that time, human beings believed in God and a Saturn reality. Now, through the acceleration of technology, people believed in the power of their minds as creators.

If we track the development of modern medicine, we find acceleration of medical discoveries since the discovery of Neptune. It ushered in all kinds of vaccines, and isolated different chemical components within the body, and then produced a synthetic version to supplement our deficiencies. Homeopathy originated which used herbs as whole health foods. Funny thing is, it may all be an illusion because you never see the ingredients growing or being processed. We see a projected form of something as a liquid or pill and believe in a scientific process that we are consuming its essence in whatever form we receive.

Pluto's Generational Impact

Pluto is the last object discovered in our solar system, originally considered a planet. Referred to as the dark planet, Pluto represents the end of our organic life. Its energy comes at the end of the outer planetary world, after Jupiter, Saturn, Uranus, and Neptune. Because of its size and density, Pluto's properties are more in alignment with the inner planets than with the outer planets. This paradox is what has created the astrological archetype of Pluto being the angel of death and transformation. Pluto represents the end; it is where the dream dies, and we reawaken to a new birth, a new form, and a different way of organizing our perception of life.

Since the discovery of Pluto in 1930, its energy has brought wide spread corrosion to many of our national, cultural, and religious traditions, including the redefinition of our values and morals, which has altered the nature and significance of marriage, family, birth, children, and gender roles. We have created nuclear and chemical weapons of mass destruction. This has changed the balance of power from large countries to radical, terrorist organizations having the potential to destroy human civilization. Technical devices have turned the organic world into a psychological playground. This has led to the reduction and elimination of many species and a significant shift in our orientation to sex and human reproduction. There has been rapid industrialization of the globe, threatening the Earth's atmosphere, Waterways, and vegetation. This is significantly affecting our relationship with the Earth.

Humans must consciously alter how they have organized their perceptions and relationships with each other. This consciousness is following a revolutionary wave of rapid global communication and connectivity, giving rise to consciousness without human form. This allows our minds to connect without organic interpretation. It also enables us to connect and unite with one another without having to nationally, culturally, racially, or by gender justify and validate the interaction. We are making unions with machines, devices, and technology for security. As an organic being, people can no longer rely solely on human-based interactions to interpret reality or security.

Here, are some of the worlds Pluto has altered since its energy manifested here on Earth. From its discovery in 1930, until 1939, Pluto was in the sign of Cancer, which altered the home, family, and traditional security. Family responsibility for the elderly began its decline as the Social Security Act of 1935 increased the opening of private "Old-Age" homes. From 1939 to 1958, the Pluto in Leo generation altered our perception and usage of sex, and brought a new perspective of individualism, new machines, devices, and technologies. From 1958 to 1972 Pluto in Virgo stopped individuals from following the way of their parents. It was the beginning of society changing after generations, to altering within generations. From 1972 to 1984 Pluto in Libra brought death to the traditional social choices of relationships. It started with the structure of relationships, the longevity of relationships and increased the number of choices that were sexually and romantically available.

From 1984 to 1995 Pluto in Scorpio, accelerated the end of traditional commitments and exposed us to a variety of ways of life. The rise of abortions ended commitment to the unborn fetus, AIDS brought death through sexuality, and we began a commitment to the non-human world of the computer. The Information Age epitomized this trend by the Internet hitting a critical mass in the early 1990's.

From 1995 to 2008 PLUTO in Sagittarius saw a shift in our belief systems. Traditional education started reconstruction. There was a new global redefinition and the beginning of new religious wars. Pluto entered Capricorn in 2008 where it will be until 2023. We have already begun to see the elimination and transformation of external structures that we relied on in the past such as corporations and jobs, governments, political affiliations and laws.

Pluto is transforming the way we have organized and approached our lives. It will challenge those who do not have the structure, tools, technology, or knowledge to function, without some distress. Wherever Capricorn shows up in your Solar Map you are being pushed to reorganize by a larger structure that defines reality through obligation and duty. Between now and 2023 Saturn in Capricorn will test your ability to restructure, reorganize and operate by proficiencies. From this point on, it is about taking responsibility.

Acceleration and adaptation is the mode of this Post-Plutonic era, in almost all areas of our lives. Those who cannot will be obsolete, finding fewer safety nets to buffer their fall. The emphasis is now on technology, economics, and consumerism, which is creating a more stressful, competitive and separating experience on a humanistic level. Our worlds are changing at a rapid rate. Those holding on to the old ways may find themselves obsolete.

The Signs and Their Corresponding Planetary Energy

ARIES / TAURUS / GEMINI / CANCER / LEO / VIRGO and LIBRA operate from an inner planetary orientation and behavioral perception, where the physical body's feelings dictate reality. This energy operates by awareness, perceptions, feelings and the five senses and one's processing forms conclusions about what one sees. This is the world "as is". These signs belong to the physical body, which is part of the dense world of form. They represent what the body experiences and where internal urges direct actions. "I have a feeling inside of me that causes a reaction within me, and I expect another person to be responsive to reduce the degree of tension and stress that these internal sensations are causing me." They belong to the organic world, which bases reality on its form, and form operates by: reaction, responses, fear and a lot of emotionalism.

Extensive exposure to SCORPIO energy has led to the conclusion that it reflects the asteroid belt of discombobulated matter as well as Pluto energy. Scorpio breaks down and rebuilds as part of the transformation cycle. It has a combination of inner planetary physical feeling energy, along with the outer planetary energy of consciousness, which drives its need for giving and receiving commitment. An abundance of Scorpio energy must be vigilant against behavior that locks into believing it is deprived and can not receive, therefore, distrust, and disbelief is the approach.

SAGITTARIUS / CAPRICORN / AQUARIUS and PISCES is outer planetary energy, where one must go beyond the five senses to the world of thought and creativity. Once we get to the social signs, we interact with the world through beliefs and ideas more than the physical body. The skills in this dimension are to be able to create discipline over the body, to define, articulate, assess and contextualize another person, situation and circumstance.

When the chart has more planets in outer planetary signs, the individual is a component serving society, or relying on creativity more than accepting how things appear to be. The outer planets are similar to the cold, polar-regions on the Earth, which are not conducive for life. Thought must come in to recreate the environment. This energy creates artificial life and artificial warmth. Aquarius and Pisces are from the realm of the unseen world that has a vision to create reality as it can be. It does not just exist in "what is".

The SOLAR BODIES and Their Energy			
Solar Body/Planet Influence	Signs It Governs	House Ruler-ship	Characteristics
SUN Inner Planetary	LEO	5th	• Identity and individuality • Ego • Determination • Main direction and focus • Our core personality source
MOON Inner Planetary	CANCER	4th	• Emotional self • How we relate and respond to people and situations • Our sense of home • Our Mother.
MERCURY Inner Planetary	GEMINI & VIRGO	3rd and 6th	• How we think and communicate • Our manual dexterity
VENUS Inner Planetary	TAURUS & LIBRA	2nd and 7th	• The energy we carry into relationships • Values and preferences • Pursuit of pleasure • Love, beauty and social attitudes

continues »»

The SOLAR BODIES and Their Energy			
Solar Body/Planet Influence	Signs It Governs	House Ruler-ship	Characteristics
MARS Inner Planetary	ARIES	1st	• How we express our physical energy and efforts • Self assertive • Initiating energy
JUPITER Outer Planetary	SAGITTARIUS	9th	• The energy of knowledge, beliefs, teaching and religion • Definition and conversion • Optimism and aspirations • Areas of expansion • Jupiter disciplines and conditions us
SATURN Outer Planetary	CAPRICORN	10th	• Laws, boundaries, structure • Restrictions • Roles, responsibility • Obsessive and compulsive drives • Our Father • How we measure reality

continues »»

The SOLAR BODIES and Their Energy			
Solar Body/Planet Influence	Signs It Governs	House Ruler-ship	Characteristics
URANUS Outer Planetary	AQUARIUS	11th	• Creativity, ideas • Technology • Things we add to our lives • Social status • Personal and social freedom • Upheaval and unpredictability
NEPTUNE Outer Planetary	PISCES	12th	• Visionaries • Collective oneness • Dreams • Imagination • Deceptions, illusions • Drugs • Projection • Remote viewing
PLUTO Asteroid Belt and Outer Planetary	SCORPIO	8th	• Power and control • The ultimate lesson in life • Transformation of self and others • Death and rebirth • Regeneration and healing

Chapter Three

Elements

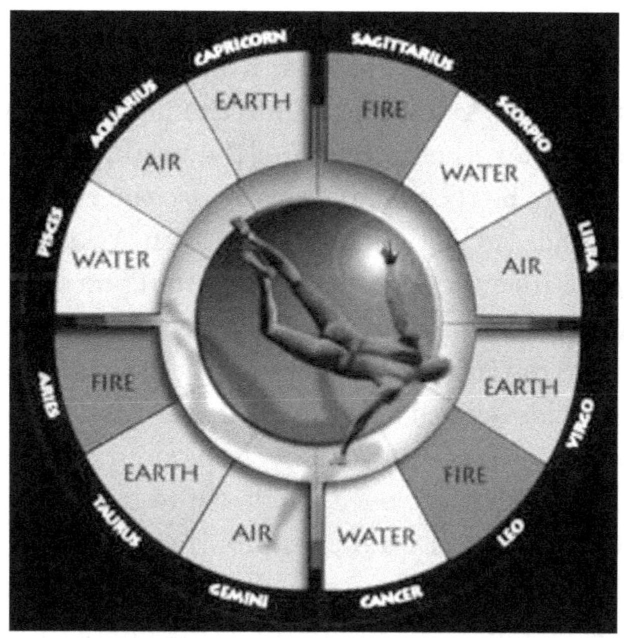

Each sign represents one of the following elements:

Fire Earth Air Water

Fire sign people (Aries, Leo and Sagittarius) needs to do something. They are predisposed to act. The Water hierarchy (Cancer, Scorpio and Pisces) utilizes the body to feel and emotionally connect. The Earth hierarchy (Taurus, Virgo, and Capricorn) structures and organizes the body to stabilize themselves and others. The Air hierarchy (Gemini, Libra, and Aquarius) have an intellectual orientation and try to seek some perceptive agreement. Each elemental hierarchy is evolving the physical being and reorganizing those basic energies with a progression that can increase the consciousness directing the body.

Fire Lessons

Fire is the ability to act.

Fire energy needs to consume something or someone. It is exuberant and enthusiastic, often with a developed sense of self-importance. One acts to protect another person or to be protected (Aries). By acting as self, one becomes solid in their individuality (Leo). One acts to gain knowledge and merge with another through beliefs (Sagittarius).

The first Fire sign, Aries represents the need to survive at any cost. You are the true warrior, the protector of the weak, and a strong, resilient life force with which to be reckoned. Aries is also the ruler of anger, which if repressed can implode as well as explode. As an Aries, you are operating through emotional Fire energy, which means that you are taking actions to initiate a response, based on your impulses. Because your body did not perceive it received the nurturing that you needed, the only way that you can feel secure is to provide security for yourself and another person. The Aries lesson is to regulate your perceptions, actions, and anger. Aries energy is more powerful and influential, once you learn to harness the flame.

The second Fire sign, Leo represents the need to act independently and have a greater sense of self. As a Leo, you are operating through physical Fire energy, which means you are directing energy toward yourself by being individualized. Your lesson as a Leo is to learn self-commitment and how to regulate your own energy, with or without the recognition of the group. You still expect nurturing and caring, but you need to become your unique self. Dynamically your focus is on individualism—your own individualism as well as assisting others in their individualization. The Achilles heel for most Leo's is their pride, and not wanting to alter their opinions or behavior in front of others, or at the request of others.

The third Fire sign, Sagittarius represents the need for personal independence, and to express and act on one's beliefs. As a Sagittarius, you are acting through mental Fire energy, which means you are directing energy toward knowledge that you seek, and trying to get to the shared beliefs of your unions. Your lesson, as a Sagittarius is to learn to listen, even if you think you know best. Do not bail out of responsibilities because you fear confinement. Remember, Sagittarius is relationship energy, so by pursuing and dispensing information, you are constantly seeking to understand what we believe and how this dictates our behavior, what involvements we make and how we construct our commitments.

Earth Lessons

Earth is the ability to stabilize and stand independently.

Earth signs tend to assess things in terms of purpose, practicality and personal goals. It represents a degree of personal solidification where you can merge and then separate. Taurus is the beginning of an internal love of self where you can ultimately stand away from your mother. Virgo is the love of family where you can ultimately stand away from family. And Capricorn is the love of work where you can ultimately stand away from the group.

Earth energy is the physical backbone of society. With this energy, there is realism, importance placed on the five senses and preference in dealing with matters they can touch.

The first Earth sign, Taurus represents a need to regulate and stabilize yourself. As a Taurus, you are operating through emotional Earth energy which means you are directing energy toward yourself by using your own ideas, resources, habits and emotional information. Your lesson as a Taurus is to learn to stabilize yourself so that you can probe the environment without insecurity. You are seeking personal security while dynamically seeking energy from someone you can participate with and get assistance from, in completing your objectives.

The second Earth sign, Virgo represents a need to be responsible back toward the group. As a Virgo, you are operating through physical Earth energy, which means you are directing energy toward the group (family, school, church, and other institutions) by being responsible and useful. Your lesson as a Virgo is to serve without being overly critical of yourself, or others. To perfect the art of service for those who are devoted to you, especially back to the family or group that was devoted to your development. You are learning to be with others responsibly, without being consumed in the process.

The third Earth sign, Capricorn represents a need to achieve one's goals, and obtain social recognition. As a Capricorn, you are operating through mental Earth energy, which means you are refining, organizing and structuring the type of actions you use to initiate a response from others. Your lesson as a Capricorn is to learn to be a solid, independent person who can operate by beliefs within the collective. Using the principles of obligation and duty, you are dissolving into a symbolic projection by merging into one within the collective. You know love through obligation, so you tend to choose people who need your responsibility skills.

Air Lessons

Air is the ability to conceptualize and communicate.

Air has a faster rhythm than the other elements. There is a faster pace and more exploration as one gets into sync with the flow of thoughts versus merging with the body's flow of structure, feelings or actions. The Air space has a perpetuation of ideas, continuation of conversation with little interruptions. In contrast, body energies may be consumed by what they physically go through, need prompting to participate, or must confront internalized feelings and issues. Air needs social interaction and mental stimulation. It is cold and detached, comfortable with abstractions and concepts, and often seems to have their heads in the clouds.

As a Gemini, you are exploring the environment through all modes of communication, and learning how to conform to the family. Libra is relationship energy that weighs choices and seeks to be in agreement with another person. Aquarius has new and unconventional ideas and seeks to find its placement within the collective social order.

The physical Air sign, Gemini represents the first phase of consciousness, which is the ability to conform. As a Gemini, you operate through emotional Air energy, which means you are ideally directing energy toward the group by conforming and being directed by their views. Your lesson as a Gemini is to learn how to regulate your behaviors, actions, emotions, and feelings to live within social agreement. You are learning to respond to language and to direct your energy through language based on how the group has symbolized reality. The challenge is fighting the impulse to be a nonconformist.

The second Air sign, Libra represents the second phase of consciousness, which is the ability to make choices about your merging. As a Libra, you are operating through physical Air energy and initiating actions to receive from the people you have chosen. Your Libra lesson is to learn how to direct your energy based on concepts and principles. You also represent balance. You are taking the values of your family and the needs of another person, and trying to balance that into an agreement that you have chosen that warrants your responsibility.

The third Air sign, Aquarius represents the highest phase of consciousness, the ability to process through a "knowing" and incorporate many facets into a whole. As an Aquarian, you are operating through mental Air energy, using your thoughts to create reality. As a creator, you often put things together that do not naturally belong with each other. The collective, or greater social order, sets the context for what determines reality in most areas of one's life. Your lesson as an Aquarian is to learn how to operate in agreement with the collective. You are learning to direct energy toward yourself by directing energy toward the social group itself.

Water Lessons

Water produces the ability emotionally to communicate.

Water is a source of refreshment. Although it is colorless, it reflects the colors of what is in it, and what it surrounds. Incredibly sensitive to their surroundings, Water types need something as a container, in order to be regulated. Water is the conduit by which the world of devotion maintains security and connection. As we evolve and go into deeper levels of devotion, we include more people in our circle than just the original connections. We evolve from family (Cancer) to marriage (Scorpio) to the greater society (Pisces).

The first Water sign, Cancer represents the need to belong. As a Cancer, you are operating through physical Water energy. You are initiating actions to receive nurturing from those within the family or group. Your lesson as a Cancer is to learn how to regulate your behaviors, actions, emotions, and feelings to the rules of the group. Not only by emulating and conforming but also by learning the conceptual reasons for their rules. This last step is often missing.

The second Water sign, Scorpio represents the need for commitment. As a Scorpio, you are operating through mental Water energy, directing energy toward yourself by directing energy toward the person who is committed to you. Your lesson as a Scorpio is to learn to live by and within commitments, because you are seeking more than an emotional connection with another person. You are seeking to transform the relationship through commitment—based on the nature and bond of why you both are in union together.

The third Water sign, Pisces represents the need to be devoted. As a Pisces, you are operating through emotional Water energy, directing your energy toward the group through the principles of devotion and tradition. Your lesson as a Pisces is to learn to sacrifice and serve others based on your ability to stand strong for those you are devoted to, and not become a martyr in the process. With a sense of empathic love, you are the mother bird who surrenders herself to feed and train her young.

Air is the only element that exists in all things. Air carries Water, moves dirt and fuels flame. It directs our actions and emotions, so if there is no Air in a person's chart, they cannot direct their actions or emotions. Thought ultimately directs the flow of life. It can add to stability, or erode stability. It can ignite flame, or extinguish flame. In combination, Air and flame can evaporate Water and erode emotions. Air guides what life can exist and where life can exist. Earth structures life as a stabilizer. Together, Air and Earth are a medium that can balance Fire and Water. When you analyze a chart, look at how much Air and Earth show up to balance life.

FIRE ACTS	**EARTH STABILIZES**	**AIR COMMUNICATES**	**WATER EMOTIONALLY RELATES**
ARIES • Act to protect self • or others.	TAURUS • Act to stabilize self away from the source.	GEMINI • Communicate its opinions and has a need to explore.	CANCER • Bring emotional nurturing to others.
LEO • Act to individualize.	VIRGO • Act to stabilize the family.	LIBRA • Merge to be in union based on choice and agreement.	SCORPIO • Merge with others through emotional commitment.
SAGITTARIUS • Act on one's beliefs	CAPRICORN • Act to stabilize through work.	AQUARIUS • Socially communicate with an innate sense of collective agreement.	PISCES • Bring emotional devotion to the uninitiated, like the mother bird devoted to her young.

continues »»

FIRE ACTS	EARTH STABILIZES	AIR COMMUNICATES	WATER EMOTIONALLY RELATES
• 0-1 FIRE • If you are missing the element of Fire in your chart, you tend to de-stabilize the actions of others. • Try to get people to act on your behalf. There is often a lack of physical energy. • There are drives but often frustration in the process of achieving. • Operate in the social/spiritual world where one does not act as a self. • 4+ FIRE MEANS: • It is difficult to regulate your actions and society does not contain you.	• 0-1 EARTH • If you are missing the element of Earth in your chart, you merge with others to be complete. • You will seek to be in union with others for security and may lose yourself in your unions. • No Earth people have issues with money. They either mismanage money, or never feel they have enough to be secure. • 4+ EARTH MEANS: • You are very self-reliant and relationships do not contain you.	• 0-1 AIR • If you are missing the element of Air in your chart, you will destabilize the thoughts of others, and may have difficulty forming agreements. • You can be overly attached to your family for security. • No Air people usually have to experience something to determine if it is true or not. They do not like to be told and do not conceptualize first. • 4+ AIR MEANS: • You live in the thought realm and the family does not contain you.	• 0-1 WATER • If you are missing the element of Water in your chart, you will attract emotional people and live vicariously through their emotions. You have a hard time relating emotionally because people did not relate to your feelings. • You may have a hard time leaving the mother and world of devotion. • 4+ WATER MEANS: • Emotions can overwhelm you, and your mother can not contain you.

Chapter Four

Signs Represent MODES of Energy

(How the energy is expressed)

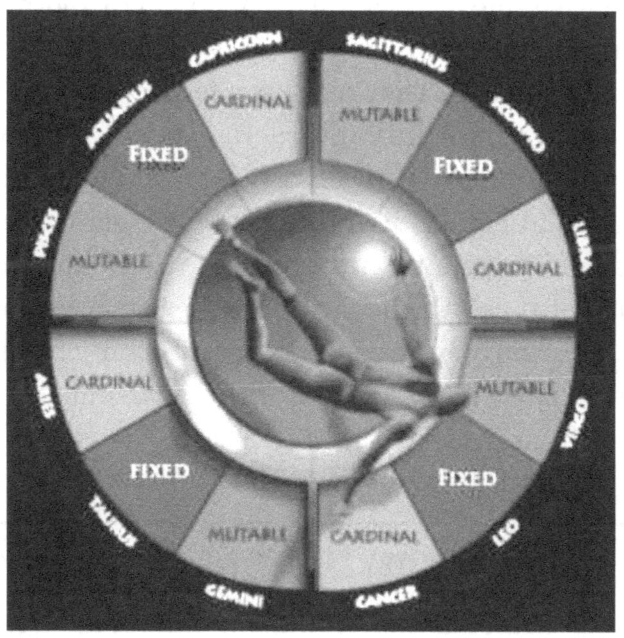

Modes of Energy

There are three prototypes of children, born into the world. First, are children who must initiate and reach out to their parents in order to receive from them. This is cardinal energy directing its actions to a source. Next, are children who do not have the ability to reach out to another person and must self-stabilize. Fixed energy tries to direct actions towards self. Lastly, there are the children who must first give of themselves to others in order to receive. This is the mutable mode operating energetically toward the group.

Cardinal Energy Is Action That Initiates A Response

Cardinal signs are strong-willed, and seek to accomplish. When you operate through a cardinal sign, you are proactively reaching out toward someone or something, in an effort to get something in return that will bring completion. However, because you are unable to guarantee a response, you tend to have opinions and judgments about the people you are involved with and your experiences.

Cardinal's positive side is the ability to respond to another. The challenge is fear of criticism and rejection. These signs will often feel rejected, not cared for, not chosen and valueless. They may seek to annihilate one's self or others, creating foundational personality disorders between what they want to receive, and the expectation of not receiving, then acting out. Often there is an inability to be in a relationship of mutuality. These signs are action oriented, attuned to crisis, and frequently jump out of the pan and into the Fire.

When they act as angels in the midst of other people's darkness, they adjust the lost souls who have been consumed, and their job is to stand between the individual and that which is attempting to consume them. As we evolve through the signs, from Aries to Cancer, Libra to Capricorn, we are reducing the variables of uncertainty to increase the probability for receiving.

Cardinal Sign	Energy	Challenge
ARIES	• Initiates to protect self, or protect others. • Initiates actions to receive, based on impulses.	• Aries can be rejected by the mother and in turn reject its sources. • If you feel rejected by your mother, you will have difficulty stabilizing away from the source and it will be difficult to conform to the group.

continues »»

Cardinal Sign	Energy	Challenge
CANCER	• Initiates people to care for them, or they must care for others. • Initiates action to become part of a group, or make others feel a sense of belonging.	• Cancer often feels rejected by the family, or rejects people in a group if they feel others do not share the same likeness. • If you feel rejection or judgment from the family, you will not be able to solidify and individualize within the family or be responsible back to them.
LIBRA	• Initiates towards people to choose them, or struggles with their choices. • Will cue others and act toward a relationship partner to experience the circle of giving and receiving.	• Libra may feel rejected in love, or rejects others in love. • If you feel rejected by your relationship, you will not be able to merge with beliefs or commitment to a union.
CAPRICORN	• Initiate to be a successful component to the work world through obligation and duty. • Adding proficiencies to be accepted and valued.	• Capricorn may be rejected by work, or be in a position that rejects others by laying- off, or firing people. • If you feel rejected by work, you will not be able to live in agreement and obligation to that social institution.

Fixed Energy Can Direct Energy To Stabilize Itself And Others

Fixed signs are more set in their ways and their views than cardinal or mutable signs. They do not quickly adapt to changes, so they try to control their realities. When you operate through a fixed sign, you expect to receive from that which you direct your energy. You may believe you can guarantee your outcome through your own efforts, and reduce the variables of receiving.

Fixed energy is steadfast with the ability to stay consistently to a path. It plays the role of stabilizing self or others. The positive energy is when one no longer needs supplementation emotionally and physically. They can then become a stable person away from the source. The patience, stamina and tenacity are assets in completing projects.

The negative or dark side of fixed energy is fighting, battles over inclusion or exclusion, and social rebellion. These signs are known to be stubborn and do not change their minds readily.

An adjustor who has mastered fixed energy seeks to help those who cannot find stability within their Taurus, Leo, Scorpio or Aquarius phases of life. They represent stabilizing others who have missed the energy they represent.

Fixed Sign	Energy	Challenges
TAURUS	• Seek to stabilize self away from the source. • Direct energy by being self-sufficient.	• They suffer abandonment issues. They fear further abandonment, or become the one abandoning others. • Tolerance and flexibility are struggles.
LEO	• Seeking individualization, recognition and to stand independent of the family as themselves. • Directing energy toward myself by being "me."	• They may suffer from lack of recognition and unable to separate from family to be themselves, or will not give others recognition.

continues »»

Fixed Sign	Energy	Challenges
SCORPIO	• Seek commitment or gives commitment to stabilize a relationship. • By directing energy to a relationship beyond emotions and feelings, there is more security.	• They may suffer from a lack of commitment by others, and/or refuse to become committed to other people. • They may not be able to stay in a committed relationship because they feel denied by others.
AQUARIUS	• Seeking social stability and to live by thought, principles and creativity. • By directing energy toward the social ideal or social group, I am able to solidify my social identity.	• They seek inclusion but may experience exclusion, or be one that excludes others. • They may become rebel-lious, or ostracized socially.

Mutable Signs Seek To Merge And Integrate Their Energy Toward The Group

When you operate through a mutable sign, you have the gift of adaptability. Its hallmark is the ability to integrate and change. The positive side of this energy represents a person who can direct the energy of themselves and others to benefit within the values, context, and agreements of a group.

Mutable energy may put energy out to be responded to, but often do not understand the laws, rules and regulations of various environments and situations. When this happens, you are punished, ostracized, persecuted or denied for not living within the agreed upon context set forth by the greater structure. As you evolve through the signs, from Gemini, Virgo and Sagittarius to Pisces, you become more selfless in your actions toward the group. The challenge is not to be so adaptable that it inhibits your own outcomes and development.

Mutable Sign	Energy	Challenges
GEMINI	• Seek to explore and communicate, while learning how to conform to the family's views. • Interested in directing the energy of others and discovering who or what will be beneficial for them.	• Get punished for not conforming to the group. • Their actions may not be authentic. Known for a tendency to be superficial, opinionated and influenced by likes and dislikes.
VIRGO	• Seeks to represent the group, and be the responsible person to the family. • Directs energy by playing roles to the group (family, school, church and other institutions.	• Get ostracized for directing energy away from the family, or group. • Known to be critical, but learned it by receiving criticism. • Seek to be useful to people, but then may resent other's dependence on them.
SAGITTARIUS	• Seeking to gain knowledge and integrate other people's beliefs. • Thirst for knowledge and freedom.	• Get persecuted for their beliefs. • May run away and escape, fearing confinement or responsibilities they do not want.
PISCES	• Bring devotion and service to others. • Directing energy toward social institutions based on the principles of selflessness and tradition.	• See oneself as a martyr, giving too much to those who do not appreciate them. • May be deceived and denied by others.

Chapter Five
Signs

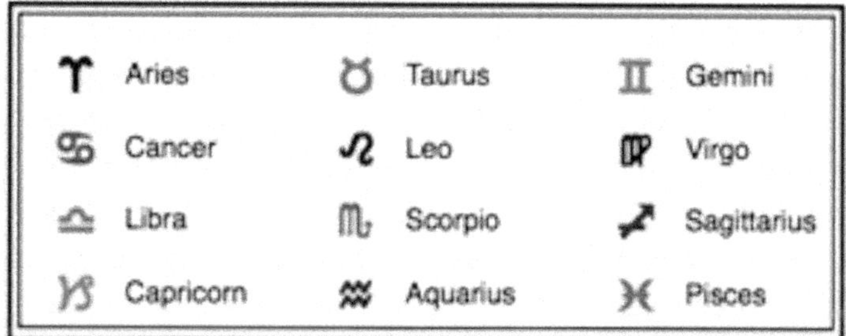

Signs

The signs the planets were in at the time of your birth reflect the planetary configuration when you were born. This is the activity in the inner part of your chart and represents the composite of energy your soul will carry to express itself. The signs represent different regions of knowledge. They demonstrate how people select and deselect information that is valuable, and where our brains tend to decode information differently. For example, an Aries would see the world differently than a Gemini. A Gemini would see the world differently than a Pisces. The energetic prototypes of the signs help you understand why people see the world a certain way. Reviewing what we have discussed so far, we can now integrate the energy dynamics with the characteristics of each sign.

SIGN	RULED BY:	ELEMENT	MODE	The 1st house placement shows:
ARIES	MARS	FIRE	CARDINAL	Where you feel you must rely on your-self

ARIES CHARACTERISTICS

Where Aries sits in the chart, is where the body comes into the game with its instinctual, behavioral, fight or flight tendencies. In childhood, you probably did not receive the nurturing you felt you needed. You adapted to this experience with a compulsive need to "do for yourself" because you do not trust relying on another person for anything. The only way you can feel secure is to provide security for another person. Having to protect yourself, you seek to protect others. In this protective mode, other people are often dependent on you, because you assist those who need protection.

Features: Active Erratic Spontaneous Leaders
High Risk Professions

- Women who don't want to play traditional "female" roles
- Understand team work more than servitude
- Will go after what you want more than trying to appease or please
- Unresolved Aries energy can become angry, combative and subject to outbursts
- Known to be strong willed, competitive and a "fighter" for what you want

SIGN	RULED BY:	ELEMENT	MODE	The 2nd house placement shows:
TAURUS	VENUS	EARTH	FIXED	Income, values, natural talents, possessions, and how you stabilize yourself

TAURUS CHARACTERISTICS

Where Taurus sits in the chart is where you stabilize yourself and are resourceful and independent in getting your needs met. You have a compulsive need for physical security – whether it is your money, home, relationships or family. Once you make up your mind, you do not like changes, and you do not like letting go of possessions. You are practical, pragmatic and often bound to the material world.

Features: Fears of abandonment Sensual Relies on self Stubborn Possessive

- Like to be connected but independent
- Prudent with resources
- Structures self and others
- The physical comforts and pleasures of life are important
- You do not like to take risks and prefer things that build towards security

SIGN	RULED BY:	ELEMENT	MODE	The 3rd house placement shows:
GEMINI	MERCURY	AIR	MUTABLE	Exploring and interacting with the environment. How you process ideas. Communications.

GEMINI CHARACTERISTICS

Where Gemini sits in your chart, is the area you bring exploration, communication, opinions about what you like and dislike, and nonconformist behavior. Gemini's are able to verbally respond to others, and direct energy through language. You compress your experiences into a concept, and communicate how your internal world perceives reality.

Features: Non-conformists Talkative Opinionated Bored Easily Sense of humor

- Likes to delve into many different things and needs freedom
- Mutable views that change frequently
- Double natured and hard to be consistent
- Not always mature enough to totally sacrifice to another
- Often separate from people in the need to explore something else
- Defines the world relative to self and redefines things to have a better image of self

SIGN	RULED BY:	ELEMENT	MODE	The 4th house placement shows:
CANCER	MOON	WATER	CARDINAL	Your home and early childhood. Nurturing energy, and where one seeks to belong.

CANCER CHARACTERISTICS

Where Cancer shows up in your chart, is where you are home for others, and where you seek to belong. It represents initiating emotions and nurturing to be cared for, or to care for others. There is often a duality to the Cancer energy; you can be indiscriminate in getting nurturing from others, yet highly selective about who you feel belongs with you. Here is a person overly sensitive, caring for others, responsive to others, seeking belonging, yet not being responded to themselves.

Features: Nurturing Emotional responsiveness Protective of loved ones Caretakers

- Struggle with their sense of belonging and therefore try to make others belong
- Self protective when things are uncomfortable and can harbor insecurities
- Addictive patterns because it is hard to get needs met from their family
- Home environment is very important
- Not overly social, there needs to be some solitude time
- Can be overly sensitive, moody, and hold on to emotional hurts
- Perceives criticism and imaginary insults that may not be real
- Procrastinates and is reactive to being told what to do

SIGN	RULED BY:	ELEMENT	MODE	The 5th house placement shows:
LEO	SUN	FIRE	FIXED	As a Leo, you are acting to become your individualized self. You require praise, recognition and to be unique.

LEO CHARACTERISTICS

Where Leo shows up in the chart is where you need recognition, where you express your individuality, and where you assist other people to individualize. Through your creative pursuits, you seek to get to the core of your unique potential. In relationship, you need recognition and caring, but you also need some space because there is a need to be "me."

Features: Creative Proud Expressive Dramatic Courageous Vain Self involved

- Likes to be the center of attention, which is why there are a lot of Leo actors
- There is a natural magnetism and leadership quality
- Leo energy seeks continuous reinforcement, and needs to be reassured of love and loyalty
- Need to be recognized, admired and adored. If not, the ego and pride can be disturbed
- Possess a giving and loving nature
- We often think of Virgo as the perfectionists, but Leo's also demand perfection of themselves

SIGN	RULED BY:	ELEMENT	MODE	The 6th house placement shows:
VIRGO	MERCURY	EARTH	MUTABLE	It represents our health, daily responsibilities, and serving people.

VIRGO CHARACTERISTICS
Where Virgo shows up in the chart is where you must be responsible and represent. It may also indicate where the family interjects its control over you. Virgo's are often considered the "Cinderella's" of the zodiac. **Features:** Practical Perfectionists Responsible Detail oriented Routine driven • Analytical and may ponder every detail extensively • Critical of yourself and others. • May take a long time to commit • Initially reserved • Grounded and one that others rely on • Strives to get its ideas across • Often has careers in the health field or has some responsibilities related to health • Cannot escape family and playing roles to the group

SIGN	RULED BY:	ELEMENT	MODE	The 7th house placement shows:
LIBRA	VENUS	AIR	CARDINAL	The need to merge in partnerships and relationships. Where you weigh your choices and seek to find balance.

LIBRA CHARACTERISTICS

Where Libra shows up in the chart, you bring your diplomatic skills and seek to merge. It represents where you make choices and seek agreement, whether it is through relationships, contracts, or mediation. There is a pattern of thinking life should be one way, but often experiencing reality to be quite different. Your parents verbally expressed things about the relationship that you did not experience, and this creates a dichotomy that stays with you – that reality often does not match your ideas.

Features: Idealistic Peacekeepers Romantic Indecisive Social

- Seeks balance and equilibrium
- Wants the good life
- Repressed anger, because you have a hard time expressing your feelings
- Likes parties, entertaining and beautiful atmospheres
- Always weighing options, thoroughly, before making a decision
- Needs to always perceive it has options and a choice. Do not like to be forced into anything
- Doesn't like to hurt other's feelings, so there is a tendency to tell "white lies"
- There are often separations in union, because you wind up choosing emotionally immature people
- You are attracted to those who are attracted to you and may get involved in an experience because someone is interested in you

SIGN	RULED BY:	ELEMENT	MODE	The 8th house placement shows:
SCORPIO	PLUTO	WATER	FIXED	Where you bring and seek commitment. Joint resources. Debt. Taxes. Inheritance.

SCORPIO CHARACTERISTICS

Where Scorpio shows up in the chart is where you seek to give and receive commitment. You dynamically operate as an evolved Water sign who no longer needs emotional nurturing from the source, but you carry a foundational deprivation from not having received it. You therefore seek more than an emotional connection with another person. You seek to be with someone in commitment, because that is the only way you can really gauge that someone cares for you.

Features: Fixed Views Controlling Manipulating Possessive Steadfast Healer

- Introspective, often having more conversations within oneself than with others
- Likes to delve into arenas with intensity more than superficially be in them
- Possessive and jealous in relationships, because you seek to give and receive commitment However, you get involved and transform people who may not be prepared to be in union
- You can create false identities for approval, to make people believe you're alright, even if you truly are not
- Passionate and emotionally intense about your involvements and seek a deep level of connection
- Lack of commitment from parent(s) at some point in life, and seeking that completion
- Can lash out and sting when pushed into a corner
- Intimidates others and does not easily trust
- Has the ability to manifest intentions, through fixed views and high concentration

SIGN	RULED BY:	ELEMENT	MODE	The 9th house placement shows:
SAGITTARIUS	JUPITER	FIRE	MUTABLE	The area we operate by beliefs and knowledge. Where we need freedom and independence.

SAGITTARIUS CHARACTERISTICS

Where Sagittarius sits in the chart is where you merge with others through beliefs. You come into the world with a different belief system than your parents. This becomes a dynamic you repeat in future relationships. As a Sagittarius, you are constantly in pursuit of knowledge, freedom and new experiences that are both physical and mental.

Features: Outspoken Expansive Optimistic Knowledge Seekers Lucky

- Because it is ruled by Jupiter many are teachers, or religious leaders
- Argumentative and self righteous
- Need to convert others to your beliefs
- With mutable energy, you often wind up representing other people's beliefs
- Optimistic and sees possibilities
- Loves to travel
- Adaptable, changeable and do not like routine
- Not detail oriented
- Seek to share your belief system and philosophy about life

SIGN	RULED BY:	ELEMENT	MODE	The 10th house placement shows:
CAPRICORN	SATURN	EARTH	CARDINAL	Career focus, social ambition, discipline, organizational skills and authority,

CAPRICORN CHARACTERISTICS

Where Capricorn shows up in the chart indicates your career identity, and the area of life you serve with obligation and duty. Many Capricorns had to play an adult role in the family to compensate for the missing energy of one parent. You grew up having to be responsible to yourself and the group, and learned to trust the external world as the world of ease. You seek commitment from a society based upon its consistency. Capricorn energy represents the ability to stabilize and structure self and others through work.

Features: Discipline Perseverance Ambitious Serious Business leaders

- You ground yourself through your work involvement and tend to be money-minded
- Goal oriented and striving for aspirations
- The Capricorn symbol is the goat climbing the mountain
- Seek to impress others and is socially conscious
- Capricorn energy is the world of law and structure
- Detached commitment to that which it serves
- Strives to be a proficient component to the external social/work world
- You find yourself through the inadequacy of others, and play roles to supplement and complete what others are missing

SIGN	RULED BY:	ELEMENT	MODE	The 11th house placement shows:
AQUARIUS	URANUS	AIR	FIXED	Social involvement, social status and a need for freedom

AQUARIUS CHARACTERISTICS

With Aquarius energy you were born to a group in which one or both parents were more socially driven than personally driven. Where Aquarius shows up in your chart, is where you seek your social identity. You may also be known to bring new ideas, and often unorthodox ways of being or unusual relationships. Aquarius energy represents the ability to stabilizing self and others by concepts and collective agreement. Being ruled by Uranus, you add things to life that may be unusual or non-traditional.

Features: Idea-based Detached Impersonal Visionaries Social Consciousness

- Operates more by thought and concepts
- Carries the energy of social inclusion or exclusion, and seeks to be part of the collective
- One's social identity and social affiliations
- Seeks to create through new ideas, new ways of seeing the world and expanding reality
- Different energy than the group you came from, and often choose people who can't escape their family
- Designed to add things and expand reality
- Accelerators who do not just accept the "status quo" if it does not fit your ideas
- Independent, rebellious and unpredictable

SIGN	RULED BY:	ELEMENT	MODE	The 12th house placement shows:
PISCES	NEPTUNE	WATER	MUTABLE	Where you sacrifice and serve. The unconscious parts of oneself. Dreams and illusions.

PISCES CHARACTERISTICS

Where Pisces sits in the chart, is where you seek to be devoted. It represents dissolving self to serve the uninitiated and wellbeing of others. You may have illusions and dreams in this area, because you do not understand the psychology of that house. Your family's traditions did not serve you to understand that area of life.

Features: Artistic Sensitive Sacrificial Martyr Spirituality Romantic

- There is usually an innate spiritual connection and desire beyond the physical realm
- Tunes into others on almost a psychic level
- Will annihilate themselves in an attempt to satisfy others. Tends to create a martyr complex
- Caring and sensitive souls who protect the underdog and surrender to the uninitiated
- Being ruled by Neptune you are known for fantasy, illusions, imagination and creativity
- There is a sensitivity to drugs and alcohol
- Pisces energy represents mental health, the subconscious, and the hidden elements of self
- Recreates how they think the world should be through dreams and projections
- Pisces often represents a missing father figure. Even if, he were present, his energy may have been devoted elsewhere

Twelve Levels on the Path to Consciousness

Each sign has an energetic predisposition that requires us to develop strategies in order to mature into a consciously aware adult.

SIGN	Twelve Lessons to Regulate Energy for Maturity
ARIES	• Learning how to regulate fears, compulsive behavior and sovereignty
TAURUS	• Learning how to regulate your will, possessiveness and actions
GEMINI	• Learning how to conform by regulating your scattered thoughts and behavior within a psychological construct
CANCER	• Learning how to regulate your moods, feelings and interactions
LEO	• Learning how to regulate your ego and desires
VIRGO	• Learning how to regulate your responsibilities and criticisms
LIBRA	• Learning how to regulate your choices and internalized anger
SCORPIO	• Learning how to regulate your commitments and need for control
SAGITTARIUS	• Learning how to regulate your beliefs and need for freedom
CAPRICORN	• Learning to regulate your obligations and duties
AQUARIUS	• Learning to regulate your social identity, affiliations and ideals
PISCES	• Learning to regulate your devotion to not become a martyr, and conquering your unconscious aspects of self

Chapter Six
Your Energetic Profile

Your biggest lesson in this lifetime is to master the diversified energy you were given at birth. The problem is a large portion of the energy that motivates us is stored in our unconscious. Our unconscious mind is making choices it must act out, whereas our conscious social and cultural mind is making choices it must live out, not just act out. Trying to bridge these two worlds and the distortions they create for each individual becomes the lessons and challenges that confront humanity. This energetic profile will help you recognize the multiple lives you are living, by defining the conscious and unconscious paths that are seeking completion.

In your personal inventory, there is no such thing as equality in life – just what's in your "goodie bag." We will examine your inventory of "goodies" to help you understand your strengths and challenges. And how these "goodies" have equipped you, or ill-equipped you to participate in the progressive, developmental phases of human and social life. That's right. You are preprogrammed with a set of energetic components that will determine the qualities that you as an individual has to work with, just as you were born into a situation you did not choose. You were also given unresolved unconscious information and a set of conscious requirements that you also did not choose.

Your conditioning is a combination of the energies from your biological lineage and the lineage of how your group had socially and culturally evolved and merged over time; to the roles, opportunities, expectations and boundaries placed on gender and sexual orientation. Your inventory is a composite of energies operating on the mental, physical, social and spiritual arenas, each one having different degrees of proficiency and maturity.

Male and Female Energy

When you look at an energetic profile, one of the things you must take into consideration is male and female energy. The Earth and Water signs are female and receptive, which represents a negative ground. Fire and Air signs are male energy and represent positive charges to a negative ground. Male and female energy are an interchange of positive and negative currents that need each other to compliment and complete the energetic circle.

Lets say a child is experiencing a series of negative emotions internally; he needs something positive to balance off his insides. He needs a positive charge to his negative ground. Situations are inherently neutral in and of themselves. They are an empty current until either negative or positive energy is applied to create what it is. When there is a negative space, for the current to flow you must become positive. A seed is a negative ground, or an unfertilized egg is a negative ground which needs a positive charge to grow into something else.

Male Positive Energy Fire signs are Aries, Leo, and Sagittarius

Male Positive Energy Air signs are Gemini, Libra and Aquarius

Female Negative Energy Water signs are Cancer, Scorpio and Pisces

Female Negative Energy Earth signs are Taurus, Virgo and Capricorn.

When you examine your relationships, look at how many signs are female and male, and the need of the particular male or female energy. As you dynamically interact with people keep in mind that two negatives will often produce too little movement or resolution, and two positives may wind up in blowups.

Someone with a lot of female energy absorbs the energy of others and has a more receptive energy. When there is an abundance of male energy, if it's Air then you will be continually communicating; and if it's Fire you can expect physical activity. If someone is coming to you with negative ground energy you need to provide a positive charge to balance it off. This means the negative energy is seeking a positive response or action. In contrast, if someone is bringing male energy they may require an emotional or structural response, which is considered female energy.

A female born in a positive sign (Aries, Gemini, Leo, Libra, Sagittarius and Aquarius) is often father-dominated with more of an interest in career and ideas than in traditional domestic roles. Sometimes they can seem too "bossy," intellectual, independent or career oriented. When they do have a family, they most likely also need outside interests or a career as well.

A male born in a negative sign (Taurus, Cancer, Virgo, Scorpio, Capricorn and Pisces) is usually raised in a mother-dominated situation. He is more receptive and intuitive than a positive sign man. He may not be as sure of himself around other males, and there is often a subversive quality. They are not always straight forward and assertive, because their male energy operates under the female energy. A side effect for men in negative signs is a basic lack of respect for authority figures since most authority figures are male.

Finding the Degrees in your Chart

The astrological chart has a number of symbols that represent planets, asteroids, nodes, signs, houses, and aspects. Right now, we will focus on planets and signs, and the designated number associated with them. Each number has a symbolic meaning in terms of one of the hierarchal emotional, physical and social drives. To get a basic energetic preview of how you approach life, look at the ten planets and the drive each planet symbolically represents in your psyche. Let's get a generalized energy profile so you can see how many planets need to receive; how many planets represent self stability; and how many planets represent the maturity of directing other people who are less mature than you.

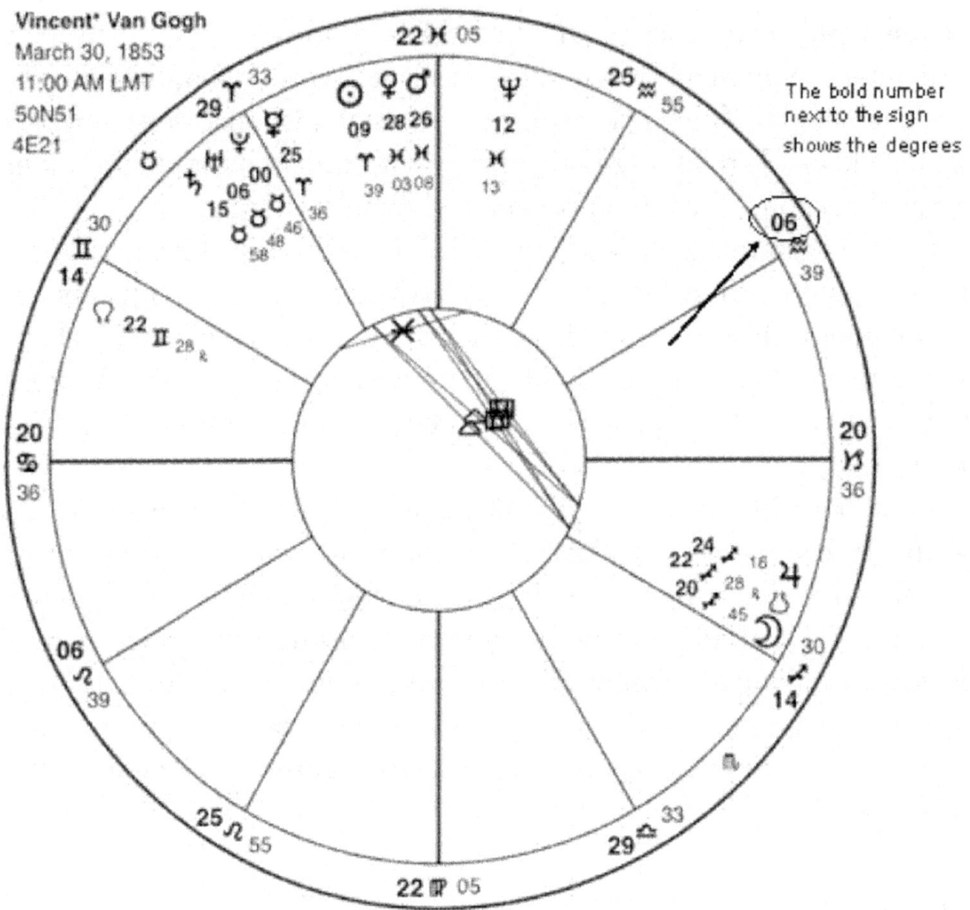

To see your energetic maturity profile take a look at your chart and write down:

Your Sun is in ____________________sign at ____ degrees

The Sun represents our identity, sense of self and individuality.

Your Moon is in ________________sign at ___ degrees

The Moon represents our emotional self and how we nurture ourselves, and others.

Your Mercury is in ______________ sign at ___ degrees

Mercury is how we think and communicate.

Your Venus is in ________________ sign at ___ degrees

Venus is the planet of love, representing self-love and the energy we carry into relationships.

Your Mars is in _________________sign at ____ degrees

Mars is how we initiate and act as well as our sexual identity.

Your Jupiter is in ________________sign at ____ degrees

Jupiter is the planet of knowledge, teaching and religion. How we define and relate to ourselves, and the world around us.

Your Saturn is in ________________sign at ____ degrees

Saturn is our obsessive and compulsive drives. It represents how we organize and structure ourselves, and the roles we play to the world around us. It is law, boundaries and measurement.

Your Uranus is in ________________sign at ____ degrees

Uranus is characterized by how we add things to our lives. It is the energy of creativity, technology, new inventions and devices. It is also our social status and group affiliations.

Your Neptune is in ______________sign at ____ degrees

Neptune is the planet of dreams, illusions, and drugs. It is the world of projection and remote viewing. It is also associated with spirituality and collective oneness.

Your Pluto is in ___________________sign at _____ degrees

Pluto is the end of the solar system and represents the end of the physical body finding completion as an organic being. Pluto represents the ultimate lesson we are here to learn in this lifetime.

Interpreting the Degrees

0-9 degrees are the CARDINAL Stage. This is initiating energy in order to establish ourselves and have people give to us or respond to us. It is also reactive energy seeking to have others operate on our behalf. The number of planets between 0-9 degrees means there are (fill in the blank) young planets that are reactive and seek to have others respond.

10-19 degrees are the FIXED Stage. One is self-stabilized, and can do things for themselves. This is responsive energy seeking to stabilize self or stabilize others. The number of planets between 10-19 degrees means there are (fill in the blank) planets that are self stabilized in which one can operate independently, respond to others and assist in stabilizing other people.

20-29 degrees are the MUTABLE Stage. With this energy, we have to do things for others. This is proactive energy directing people and seeking to bring benefit to others. The number of planets between 20-29 degrees means there are (fill in the blank) planets that are mature and can proactively direct the energy of others.

Signs and Degrees Represent an Energetic Circle

Putting the signs and degrees together gives us a better understanding of how the energy plays out. Each sign represents an energy field, and when you interface with someone you are meeting energy that is seeking to receive, to express, or give to those who can't receive.

The following highlights are simplified dynamics for each sign. This is basically a description for the Sun sign, but you can combine this to the other planetary energies as well. It is a little clue into understanding the phenomena between you and another person, the energy requirements or lessons the individual and yourself are trying to fulfill, as well as the type of relationship your energies will create.

Aries is male energy that acts for self-survival. Sometimes they act to rescue others who are unstable, and other times they are the ones who need rescuing.

The Cardinal stage 0-10 degrees: Need someone to act for me.
The Fixed stage 11-20 degrees: Need to act for myself.
The Mutable stage 21-30 degrees: Need to act for others.

Taurus is female energy that seeks to ground and structure self or others. The energy is not looking for people to take over for them, but to work with them in cooperation.

The Cardinal stage 0-10 degrees: Need someone to be of assistance to me.
The Fixed stage 11-20 degrees: Need to structure myself.
The Mutable stage 21-30 degrees: Need to be someone to assist others.

Gemini is male energy that is exploring how to direct its energy. It is either about oneself, or about others.

The Cardinal stage 0-10 degrees: Need someone to be about me.
The Fixed stage 11-20 degrees: Need to be about myself.
The Mutable stage 21-30 degrees: Need to be about others.

Cancer is female energy that needs nurturing and belonging.

The Cardinal stage 0-10 degrees: Need someone to care for me.
The Fixed stage 11-20 degrees: Need to care for oneself.
The Mutable stage 21-30 degrees: Need to care for another.

Leo is male energy that seeks recognition and others to be with me.

The Cardinal stage 0-10 degrees: Need someone to recognize me.
The Fixed stage 11-20 degrees: Need to recognize my own individuality.
The Mutable stage 21-30 degrees: Need to help others get recognition.

Virgo is female energy that is with the group through responsibility.

The Cardinal stage 0-10 degrees: Need to have someone be responsible for me.
The Fixed stage 11-20 degrees: Need to be responsible for myself.
The Mutable stage 21-30 degrees: Need to be responsible for others.

Libra is male energy that seeks to merge through choice and agreement.

The Cardinal stage of 0-10 degrees: Need to have someone choose me.
The Fixed stage of 11-20 degrees: Need to be stable with my choices.
The Mutable stage of 21-30 degrees: Need to choose others and bring relationship skills.

Scorpio is female energy that merges to be with you in commitment.

The Cardinal stage 0-10 degrees: Need to receive commitment.
The Fixed stage 11-20 degrees: Need to be committed to self.
The Mutable stage 21-30 degrees: Brings a commitment to others.

Sagittarius is male energy that merges with others through belief.

The Cardinal stage 0-10 degrees: Need to convert others to my beliefs.
The Fixed stage 11-20 degrees: Need to live by my own beliefs.
The Mutable stage 21-30 degrees: Need to operate toward others by my beliefs.

Capricorn is female energy that dissolves self through obligation and duty.

The Cardinal stage 0-10 degrees Needs to receive obligation from others.
The Fixed stage 11-20 degrees: Obligated to supply myself.
The Mutable stage 21-30 degrees: Obligated towards supplying others.

Aquarius is male energy that is part of the social order through collective agreement.

The Cardinal stage 0-10 degrees: Need to have society be about me.
The Fixed stage 11-20 degrees: Need to have a stable social identity.
The Mutable stage 21-30 degrees: Bring ideas, creativity and social inclusivity.

Pisces is female energy that dissolves self to represent tradition, devotion and collective consciousness.

The Cardinal stage 0-10 degrees: Need to receive devotion from others.
The Fixed stage 11-20 degrees: Need to be devoted to myself.
The Mutable stage 21-30 degrees: Need to be devoted to others.

If you have the majority of your planets in higher degrees (20-30) then the primary drive in life may be to give to others, either through example, teaching or direct responsibility. If one doesn't have very many planets that need to receive, it means they may have difficulty in understanding the subtleties of receiving, which will be reflected in the parental and family relationships, and subsequently will then affect adult intimate relationships.

A correlation would be the childhood phase, the puberty/adolescent stage and then the adult stage. Each stage reflects a different development of the brain. The last 30 degrees represent a mature mind, as opposed to the earlier stages, which are a developing or stabilizing mind. This is reflected in the degree of overwhelm and the type of overwhelm that may consume or paralyze the individual, and the coping mechanisms that are used to bring balance in the psyche. The young often "freak out," the self-stabilized have coping mechanisms, and the adult stage tries to bring resolution to others.

Why Analyze Your Energetic Patterns

This could be particularly helpful in adult relationships, whether they are intimate, friendship or business because it helps you see the energetic relationship models that are taking place beyond the symbolic definitions taking place. Many people may not recognize the relationship models. For example, you may think you are in a romantic relationship, but you may be approaching it energetically from a parent/child model in which your partner is incapable of being a balanced mate because they routinely need adjusting.

Chapter Seven

Rising Signs and Sun Signs

Even though the Sun is part of the universe, it has its own reality, its own system. Your sun sign reflects who you are, away from that which spawned you. It indicates the developmental stage your soul operates from in its evolvement. It represents the degree of consciousness you come into the world with, and tools you use to confront and address not only the situation of your birth, but the circumstances you encounter throughout life. Your rising sign indicates the spiritual lesson you enter the planet to explore and experience yourself.

If you look at the wheel of your chart, the rising sign sits at 9:00, the beginning of your first house. The time of birth determines your rising sign and changes every two hours. If you don't have a time of birth, you can still get a planetary reading (the signs the planets were in at birth). An exception is the moon. The moon stays in each sign a little more than two days, and you would have to check various times throughout the day to see if that changes the moon placement. *(Note: If you go back and look at Vincent Van Gogh's chart the rising sign is a Cancer.)*

The rising sign is the filter through which you see life. It is one of the first indicators of the psychological situation of your birth, the conditioning of your formative years, and the basic approach you will use to survive. This includes the relationship with your mother – including her conditioned approach to mothering; your sense of love and independence; your ability to conform and move with security; to language, and to stand away from your mother directing your energy.

Your prototypical experience creates a myth about your ability to receive from another person, and whether receiving is associated with ease or frustration. Whether you must act out to receive, pacify yourself from a lack of responsiveness, or eventually become independent because you believe others will not act for you. As you grow up, what you bring to others is often that same reactive behavior, because your myth has become a foundational belief about the world. This reactive behavior becomes an input to others and then their reaction to your input creates your perception of them, and of yourself. This cycle is usually an unseen dynamic, for many, beyond consciousness. For the young cannot see their input into a situation, or another person.

Rising Signs Indicate Prototypes

The rising sign reveals your psychological prototype. Each prototype has a conditioned mother/child infant experience that represents that prototype. We need to contextualize who your mother was in time and space because it will show the social utilization of women, her approach to emotions and bonding, and the conditioning of the child to operate as a prototype within the collective social/spiritual order. We will be discussing a lot about mother/child dynamics, and in many cases bonding deficits. Some people become defensive over their mothers and do not like that part of the description. However, you must bear in mind that we interface with many stages of motherhood as we are growing up.

Some mothers are skilled in the initial bonding phase and love to have the child close to their bodies, as long as possible, and do not separate from them for any length of time. Then when the infant becomes a toddler the separation may be extreme for the child. For others, the mother does not show up until the conversation stage, and then they shine as parents who try to talk and relate. So when we discuss the mother/child relationship we are discussing a stage, usually the first year, and this experience imprints us on a cellular and psychological level because we were too young to understand what was happening around us.

Let's say your innate experience as a mammal is to come out of your mother's womb and go to her breast. Many of us, born in an advanced society, left the womb and were bottle-fed, or separated after four to six weeks, while our mother juggled her career responsibilities. Some of us, once we became a toddler, moved from our mom to a TV or pre-school. Prior generations did not have these alternatives or technologies. These factors can dramatically affect how you see reality and the basic tool skills you develop. On a deeper level, outside of our consciousness, society is conditioning us to be more independent. In our western culture, children are conditioned and domesticated away from the bonding world, finding more completion and belonging with the technological, institutional and social world. The increase in working mothers, daycare centers, pre-school expansion and Head Start funding are all examples of this societal shift.

The dynamic maturity of both your sun and rising sign indicates the degree of technology, people, places or things that you will use to jettison yourself beyond your situational birth.

If your Sun Sign is Higher or Lower than your Rising Sign

If your Sun Sign is lower than your rising sign, you may have been overwhelmed by your initial experience, and that is a conditioned response you will repeat with future situational experiences. It shows that you may not have the tool structure to mature beyond the situational identity at birth, and the dynamic approach your mother had about life will seek to convert you to represent her psychology.

If your Sun Sign is higher than your rising sign, you have elevated tools to overcome the situational world of your birth. Around age seven, you will start to create a different reality than the one you had with your family.

If you know your rising sign and sun sign, you will notice that you exhibit traits of both signs. The rising sign is the impression people have when they first encounter you. The sun sign is a deeper reflection of your true personality traits, those who know you can identify. It is best to become familiar with the prototypes of both your sun sign and rising sign because you embody characteristics of both.

Aries Prototype

An Aries prototype will act for self-survival. That is one of the reasons you are often a leader. Your independent streak is mainly because you did not feel your mother, or family, responded to you as a child. As infants, we need our feelings and physical discomforts responded to immediately, or else we become frustrated. Aries prototypes go through physical agitation because, as a child, you perceived no one responded quickly enough to resolve your discomfort and distress. This created a personality within you who has a compulsive need to act for yourself.

Most Aries prototypes feel misunderstood in some way by their mother, and unable to find a sense of unconditional bonding from their family. There is a likelihood you will pull away from the people you are involved with because you don't trust depending on other people providing for you. You are behaviorally reactive, internalized and need to monitor your conclusions because there is a tendency to make up stories about what is happening to you to fit your psychology. You may have a persistent need to receive from others, so you can find some form of completion. Part of your spiritual lesson is to protect others, who like yourself were left unprotected in some way. Even as a child and later as an adult you will often act to be the protector of your parent(s) in some way.

Taurus Prototype

As a Taurus prototype, you come into the world experiencing some form of abandonment. This means that once you stabilized yourself physically as a child, and started to crawl around, you were no longer able to access or recognize the emotional support and responsibility from your parent(s).

Most Taurus prototypes, were forced to be independent, away from the mother before they were ready to be separated. That is why you fear abandonment, and why isolation is your greatest punishment. You compensated for emotional dependency by becoming responsible to your mother, and security came from Mom relying on you. That pattern continues into adulthood where you will create, or find situations where others will rely on you, and that becomes your sense of security within the relationship. You do not know the connection just for who you are, you believe you must bring something to the other person. It also creates a person that has a hard time properly assessing the emotional capacity or connection of your personal involvements.

Taurus as a fixed sign represents stability and steadfastness. As an Earth sign, you have the ability to stand on your own, away from the source, but still need to know the source is close. This often creates an independent/dependent personality. As a Taurus, you define yourself by the experiences and inputs you receive. You seek input and positive feedback about yourself from the people who are emotionally close to you because you did not get a lot of that growing up. As part of your spiritual lesson, your soul is becoming the one others can count on, as you take on those who like yourself were abandoned in some way.

Gemini Prototype

As a Gemini prototype child, you probably had difficulty conforming to the views of your parent. As a soul, you came to the planet unable to have a parent who consistently acted for you or toward you. While still living within the environment of your parents, you probably began to explore your independence away from your parents at a very early age, before you had the maturity to do so.

Unable to find a consistent source, most Gemini prototypes had a mother who was still exploring herself, and was not clear about how to direct her own energy. You then separate from yourself by your inability to direct yourself to people and things that would benefit you. You had to direct your own energy and not count on the family. You have a compulsive need to explore the immediate environment and different forms of communication, often expressing likes and dislikes, opinions, feelings, perceptions and experiences. Your soul in this lifetime is trying to master conformity and how to direct energy toward completion. As part of your spiritual lesson, your soul tends to choose people who have difficulty directing their own energy – and you are here to guide and help direct them.

Cancer Prototype

As a Cancer prototype, you are no longer seeking a parent, and you are not overly focused on your relationship with your mother. You are exploring and experiencing the family, seeking to receive validation of caring and belonging. From this foundation, you emotionally relate, and nurture people to make them, and yourself, feel part of the group. Your sense of not belonging is a dynamic from childhood that would replicate itself in future group dynamics.

Many people with Cancer prototype childhoods had difficulty taking on the coloration of the people they came from, and learned to emulate to belong. You may be struggling with an inability to understand deeper levels of connection beyond fitting in through emulation. It is a constant struggle to belong. Cancers, often extremely connected to their family, are clannish about who belongs or does not belong with the family.

As a cardinal sign, you initiate actions in order to receive. You will initiate to receive emotional nurturing or emotionally nurture others in order to belong. Cancer prototypes bring their mother back to her original family, and allow her to receive from them due to their birth.

The first quadrant (houses 1,2,3) should not have Water in it. If you are a Cancer, Scorpio or Pisces rising it means you did not receive the emotional energy from the devoted source as much as you had to bring emotions to the source. You eventually separate from the source that you're involved with, and there is a tendency to attract people who are either overly stuck belonging to the family structure they come from, who belong to other people and can't separate from them, or who choose to belong with other people. As part of your spiritual lesson, your soul is exploring being part of the group, without separating from them because you fear that you won't belong. You tend to attract people with belonging issues and assist them to be part of the group, by bringing spiritual intervention to disconnected people or family structures.

Leo Prototype

Leo prototype children need a lot of attention and recognition, often resorting to extremes to be noticed. Most children with this sign were born when their mother was exploring her sexuality, and not yet mature enough to have responsibility skills. You then carry this energy of sexuality and individuality as you approach life, and you are learning how to solidify all your dynamics into a responsible individual for self. You are learning to be your own person who can do things on your own, without needing to rely on your parents, but you still need to be part of the group.

Part of your set up comes from a disconnection with family. You do not identify yourself with the family because your individuality is different. Family is just a landing strip on your path to self-actualization. As a fixed Fire sign, a Leo prototype stabilizes itself by its actions. That is why it seeks individualization, and to assist others on this path. The outward expression is that of the dramatic, creative, proud person who seeks recognition. As part of your spiritual lesson, your soul is exploring its own individuality, sexuality and uniqueness as a member of the group, yet separate from the group. You will tend to attract and assist others who are also on this same journey for individuality. Friendships are crucial, and you tend to develop external social families, beyond your original group.

Virgo Prototype

Virgo prototypes come to the planet at the highest level of organic conditioning. You come into the world with some deep understandings of sacrificing self for the betterment of others. You are also mature enough to represent the values of the group.

As a Virgo prototype, most came in missing your childhood. Your dependencies are not catered to because you have roles to play. You have become part of the support system within the family structure. As a Virgo, there are obligations and duties to the parent, particularly the mom, who for some reason was unable to fulfill all of her responsibilities without your assistance.

This dynamic means you are meeting a mom who never learned responsibility skills for her self. She was busy being responsible elsewhere. You then do not find that from her, so you must be responsible for yourself. As a mutable Earth sign, you operate as a stabilized self able to direct your energy, and others within the group, as a responsible component that can represent the values of the group. As part of your spiritual lesson, your soul may have assumed so much responsibility within the family that you have a difficult time ever leaving. You may also have a tendency to choose people who project themselves as being independent, but who are truly dependent. Your role then is to serve and be responsible for their development.

Libra Prototype

Libra prototypes need to be in a relationship, but are learning how to make choices that will lead to commitment. You often want others to commit to you first. This prototype represents the ability to create relationships with others through choice and agreement. The dilemma is that Libra seek to experience the ideal they have about relationships, unfortunately, many fall short.

Many people with Libra Prototype come into the world perceiving that their parents did not choose to be with each other. Or, that their parent's choices created an environment which was not balanced. Most of the time the mother could not surrender herself to her partner because she did not choose to be in life the same way, or the relationship had to make choices around your birth. Right from the start, you are trying to understand the nature of a choice within relationships. You see your parents in a relationship, but not operating cooperatively with each other. They may have spoken a lot about the nature of what their relationship is, or could be, but they physically and emotionally found it difficult to live within that construct.

You experienced a world that made choices without a commitment, and this becomes a repeated pattern you are trying to understand, resolve and mature beyond. As part of your spiritual lesson, your soul is assisting others to be in relationship through choice, but your own disillusionment about relationships and their inability to meet your expectations may make it difficult for you to get to the next stage of commitment.

Scorpio Prototype

The Scorpio prototype has to be committed towards others, often at the cost of your own identity, and more than you can find a person committed or regulated to your emotional needs. There may have been issues around your birth and an unstable situation for your mother, causing her to be committed to herself, more than to you. You then had to make a commitment to her and take on a certain amount of responsibility for her. Through your dedication and responsibility to others, the Scorpio prototype says, "I'm committed to you at the cost of my own identity."

As a Scorpio prototype, you mastered the ability to make a choice, and now you are learning how to be committed to making your choices work. Most likely, you came into a family structure where your parents – physically, emotionally, philosophically, psychologically or spiritually were unable to agree with, accept, or be committed to each other, or you. As a fixed sign, you stabilize to operate away from the family.

As a Water sign, you seek emotional commitment and bring emotional commitment. Similar to the Cancer prototype, there should be no Water in the first quadrant, so if you are a Scorpio Rising you most likely had to bring emotional commitment to the mother more than it was received. As part of your spiritual lesson, your soul is exploring the circle of commitment –

giving, not giving, receiving, and not receiving. You serve emotionally deprived people and tend to interface with those who did not receive the commitment they wanted from their family. Your journey in this lifetime is to move beyond your internal desire structure, which seeks commitment, to give a commitment.

Sagittarius Prototype

Sagittarius prototypes are born into a situation that was chaotic. Your pattern then is to attract chaotic people to assist in their development and completion. Your social archetype comes in as spiritual intervention, taking on the issues of other people.

The initial conditioning of a Sagittarius prototype has parents who seek to raise them more by beliefs than emotions. Most Sagittarius rising people, at some point, wind up having a different set of beliefs than their mother. You had to serve your mom's beliefs for security, so you wind up serving the beliefs of your relationships. You will try to convert people to your beliefs, or you may become converted to represent other's beliefs.

You live in an environment surrounding correct behavior and activities forced on you because of guilt. At some point, people are judgmental of you, so you become a judgmental person. You operate by beliefs because that is the only thing you can trust.

Your intrinsic drive relates to others through your beliefs, and when you take on unions you wind up having to be self reliant. That becomes a struggle because even though you don't want to continue this behavior, you select people that are too immature to bring responsibility skills to the union. You are no longer operating as an organic, physical being. Ideally, your belief system dictates your commitment and consistency outside of whatever you are physically or emotionally experiencing.

Persecution and punishment is the lesson you are here to learn. If you do not share the same beliefs as those you try to receive from, they will persecute you. You may repeatedly fear punishment because the physical body is on guard based on the persecution from the family for having different beliefs. In your spiritual lesson, you become responsible for immature people who are still living in the internal world – those dominated by the physical, emotional and family phases of development. Your journey is to operate toward others responsibly through a consistent set of beliefs.

Capricorn Prototype

A Capricorn prototype indicates that your parents put an emphasis on work. Your parents valued obligation and duty over bonding, and you tend to replicate this behavior. As a Capricorn prototype, you play a role to the external social order (the world outside of the family) as a component who is independent and who operates through detached commitment, discipline and responsibility. You may have bypassed your childhood altogether, believing you must be obligated to yourself and family more than they had the ability, based on the situation, to be obligated to you.

Most Capricorn prototypes play a role to the family due to one of the parents not consistently supporting or participating in the family. You then had to find your own way, to develop tools to serve or play roles where you could bring something back to the group. This cardinal Earth energy initiates actions socially, as a stable component responsible for self and others. The Capricorn personality is a workaholic, who is status conscious and socially aware, but you believe your efforts are unappreciated and taken for granted.

As part of your spiritual lesson, your soul is exploring obligation and duty based upon a belief system versus your involvement with others based mainly on bonding and connection. You choose weaker people to deal with because people look for you to stabilize them.

Aquarius Prototype

An Aquarius prototype has some separation from the biological family during their childhood. Someone may have been ill, hospitalized, or relatives may have had to step in and assist. Because of separation, the family sees you and hears you, but they do not internally understand you. Your life is a series of "situations," and you will retain this energy and respond to events as a situation, not always personally. Some may interpret this approach as being detached or cold, but often the sun sign or other elements in the charts soften it.

An Aquarius trait combines things that normally do not go together, increasing the likelihood you will choose people different from your family. This prototype comes into the world with a social awareness. There is often a rebellion against the family's social order, and a tendency to examine collective beliefs about social inclusion and exclusion. Fixed Air energy, you are solidifying as an individual within society, not just a component in obligation and duty (the Capricorn stage), but through a sense of being part of the collective.

We find that quite often the Aquarius prototype mother was supporting her husband's social advancement rather than pursuing her own. He was a person in society, and your mother had to be devoted to him. He supplied the family, but she had to take care of and rely on herself while still being devoted to his social identity. When you get in a relationship that is what you are going to do. You then may replicate supporting your partner's social advancement, but eventually you seek to have your own social identity.

You do not come to the planet to have emotional support. You came in too advanced and accelerated. As part of your spiritual lesson, you are exploring your placement in the family's social order versus the social identity you seek to actualize. Being in the first house is a challenge because one wants devotion from the family, but is often making different social choices than the group.

Pisces Prototype

An individual with Pisces prototype is examining the world of devotion. Instead of receiving devotion from your mother, you may have had to be the one devoted to her. In your initial conditioning, your mother was psychologically unavailable. Whatever society projected about the traditional mom, your mother was not that. Through some situation or circumstance, you could not access her, as a traditional mother. She was a mystery to you as you were growing up. Maybe she still is today.

A Pisces prototype often experiences the family in some form of decay and not served by society, or the collective. It then becomes difficult for you to understand the psychology of the collective, the group and the mother. You live through the family's tradition or rituals, more than bonding.

Since you were not able to receive devotion passively, you never had an opportunity to be dependent, which means you would have to be independent of the parent because you couldn't count on them. Due to your innate sensitivity to others, that dynamic would make you more docile in terms of surrendering yourself to the needs of another person. Consequently, throughout life you will find yourself often surrendering yourself to assist other people in their development. You may have a hard time understanding the psychology of the people, or groups you're involved with and may serve them more than intuitively understand them.

If you are a Pisces rising and have Water in the first quadrant, it means you had to bring devotion to your mother more than receiving devotion from her. Your pattern then will dissolve yourself to be emotionally responsive and devoted to the uninitiated, even if you replicate your mother's dynamic of not receiving devotion in return.

As part of your spiritual lesson, you are learning to be devoted to yourself and stop reeling from a lack of devotion from others. This prototype has spiritual maturity that will attract immature souls who need devotion, and you must realize that these same people are not mature enough to give devotion back. Different people intersect your circle of giving and receiving. As you get older, you will discover that those you take on to help should not be the ones you choose for a relationship.

As human beings, we all start out seeking warmth and connection. If you have a lower prototype sign (Aries - Virgo, and to a lesser extent also Libra and Scorpio) it is physically based, which means your body dictates your interpretations, and it becomes difficult to deal with the cold because you suffer. If you are un-evolved, you believe no one dealt with you and you carry hurt and pain into other human relationships. You carry the coldness with you as a context. This is when interactions and relationships become cold, situations and transitions, in life, are unwelcoming.

The only way to go beyond breakdown is to go to beliefs. You cannot use your experience as truth or the body's perception as reality. If you do, you are through because you will replicate this drama over and over, and over again. If your prototype is that of Sagittarius, Capricorn, Aquarius or Pisces, ruled by the outer planets, you have belief systems that will help you cope with the cold. You do not stay in the experience of being cold. You go some place else, or create something to deal with the cold.

Chapter Eight

Quadrants and Houses

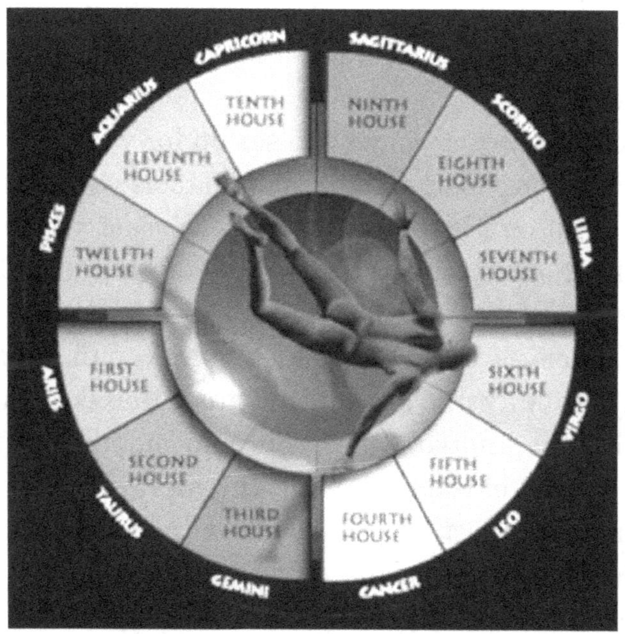

In our path to maturity, we go through phases of devotion, conformity, responsibility, beliefs, obligation and duty. There are worlds that people perceive reality from and construct their underlying psychologies around, and they become relationship models we use to interact with one another. The astrological chart shows what phase you are trying to evolve through versus the phase utilizing you, and the discrepancy or balance between the two.

There are Four Phases of Human and Social Life We all Must Develop Through

Human beings have developmental stages, stepping-stones or building blocks to growth and maturity. There are four distinct evolutionary phases and our progress requires us to take on different forms and master different energies.

The first phase is FORMULATION through devotion. The first set of energies you must master are those that formulate you as an organic and instinctual being because the physical body's muscular and skeletal structure is in a state where it cannot master the gravitational pull of the Earth. As an utterly helpless person, you are reliant on the degree of passivity you receive from your mother, or another source devoted to your development and maintenance.

In life, the first quadrant shows the set up for your approach to life, the underlying information constructing you, and tools you use to get your needs met. In the formulation phase, your ability to trust your mother matures you into an adult who is trustworthy as a devoted supplier. This is Houses 1, 2, 3 of the chart.

The second phase is SOLIDIFICATION through conformity. In this phase, you seek to solidify into a stabilized muscular/skeletal physical being. This world structures and solidifies you as a member of the family. You learn to belong as part of the group and the hierarchy of energy goes from having an emotional connection to being an individualized part of the group, then responsible back to the family. The foundation of this world is conformity. If you do not master this principle, you will experience being punished, and ostracized within the family and other social settings. In the solidification phase, your ability to conform matures you into a person who can participate positively within a group. This is Houses 4, 5, 6 of the chart.

The third phase is MERGING through responsibility. You are now evolving into a conceptual being that starts to merge with others through consciousness. You are no longer in family, and you have a need to connect with another person through choice and agreement, commitment and beliefs. As one solid person merging with another solid person, you seek to have agreements about how you direct your energy to create reality together. In this world, you begin to dissolve your individual selves to represent the union. This is Houses 7, 8, 9 of the chart.

Your ability to be responsible matures you into a person who can participate positively in relationships, partnerships and unions. The fourth phase is DISSOLVING through beliefs. Ultimately you learn to dissolve your personal sense of self to represent something other than yourself. You are a symbolic being, who becomes a component, worker, facilitator and servant to the social and spiritual world. The foundation used to direct energy is that of beliefs, obligation and duty, devotion and consciousness. This is Houses 10, 11, 12 of the chart.

Within these four phases of human, social and spiritual mastery, there are twelve energetic principles to master in order to direct energy with maturity and consciousness. Each of these perspectives has a distinct human interactive pattern associated with it, and a relationship model that symbolizes the emotional, interactive, social and psychological energetic exchanges that are necessary to attain completion. As you develop, you will try to migrate to new regions in your brain to process physical experiences, social, interactive requirements, and any new group psychologies, imposed on you. This requires new interactive patterns, perspectives, and relationship models to obtain success in the new environments.

These models are designed to dispense and receive divergent types of energy. Developmentally, you are required to master these energies, so you can have the tools to progress to the next level of human proficiency, which is controlling the probability of outcome. If you get stuck in a phase and retain old patterns, it may dominate your interactions for security with inappropriate interpretations and perspective that may no longer have the same relevance once you migrate to new regions. For example, survival techniques and information that works in the tropics may not work in the Arctic Circle.

The interactive pattern that supported you as an infant, receiving from your mother, may not work in the group phase. What if a child cried to have its needs met, and continued to use that tool in different phases of life? That behavior will become less and less appropriate to be responded to, and it will bring another outcome, which will create emotional, psychological and interactive issues. The inability to master the energetic requirements in each phase will create internal and external traumas and crises rendering you too dysfunctional if used in the progressive environment.

There are systems added to you on a continuous basis—organically, socially, and environmentally that are perceptive filters to our views of reality. There are the systems of the physical body, emotions, actions, family, school, conformity, belonging, independence, work, group consciousness, mutuality through choice, commitment through education, training, conditioning, beliefs, obligation, creativity, the natural environment, the psychological environment, the providing environment, and so on. Each of these systems then produces a person within you who has either learned or not learned to operate and cope within the different worlds or matrixes that organize your existence. As you evolve through each system, you are dynamically seeking or giving certain types of energy. These energies mature in developmental layers as you progress on your soul's journey.

Energetic Relationship Models

It is essential to understand the energy you have not mastered, as a lack of proficiency will reduce your ability to perceive or receive the benefit of the quadrant. In the following diagram, the first quadrant is about mastering the interaction necessary for receiving devotion. The second quadrant is mastering the interactions required for belonging to the group. The third quadrant is mastering the interactions of merging with another. The fourth quadrant is mastering the necessary interactions, knowledge and behavior to be socially viable. The inability to master these energies will create distortion, a sense of loss, and a sense of failing.

The basic astrological wheel is a symbolic and philosophical representation of our soul's evolution, our past life, the situation we were born into and how we were set up dynamically to experience this lifetime. The chart is a 360-degree wheel, divided into four quadrants, further broken into thirds (called houses), which represent various principles. The quadrants and houses within them denote developmental stages and regions of knowledge that contain, represent and dispense energy with certain principles that become relationship models.

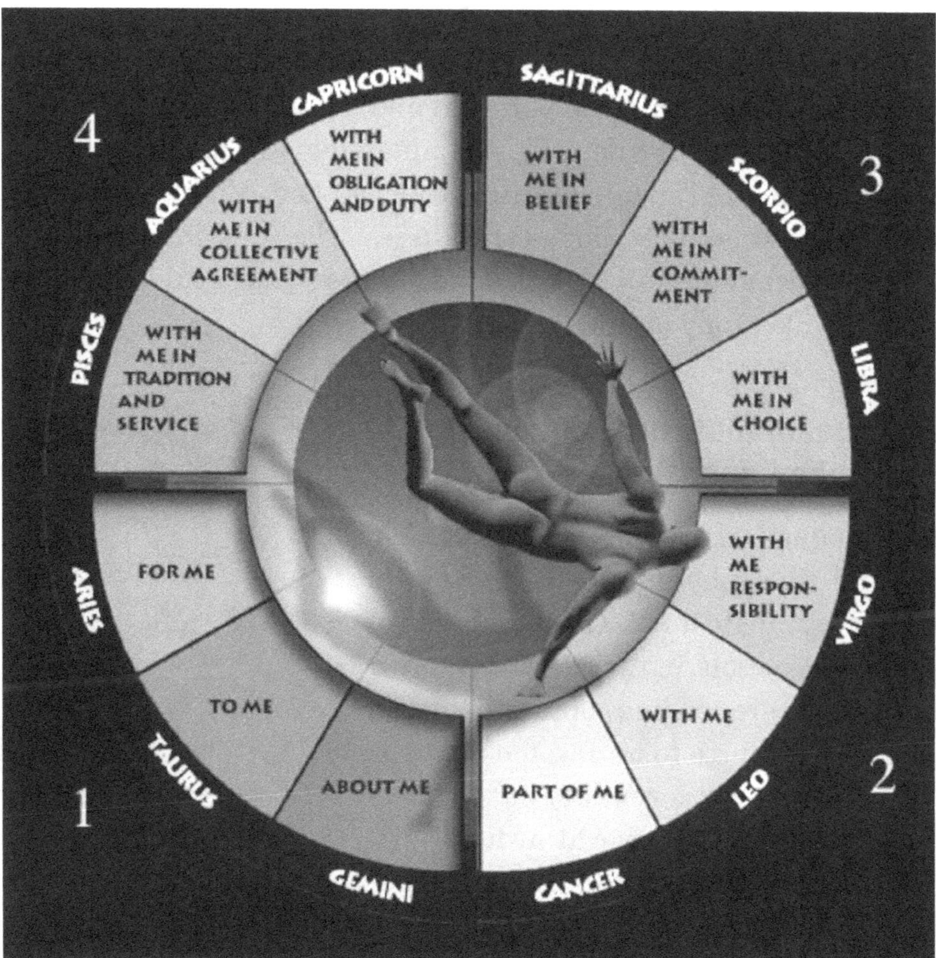

Quadrants Represent Relationship Models

Each developmental phase is represented by an interactive model such as: mother/child, parent/child, family/group, friends and organizations, relationships and labor. Each model represents a phase of energetic involvement and we are required to master these phases before we progress to the next level of human proficiency, which is to master the probability of outcome.

Each phase becomes overlaid, impacted, and reorganized by different regions of knowledge in the form of beliefs, law, machines, remote viewing, devices and even extraterrestrial information. There are different components that influence our experiences and interactions. When we look at interpreting the astrological chart, it represents fields of knowledge, behavior and experiences within the personal and social arenas of life.

Houses have natural ruler-ships dominated by the signs in the progressive order of Aries, Taurus, Gemini, Cancer, Leo, Virgo, Libra, Scorpio, Sagittarius, Capricorn, Aquarius and Pisces. The first house starts on the left side of the equator at 9:00 PM. This is where your soul is introduced to the body it will occupy on the Earth.

The First Quadrant is the Southwest Portion of the Chart (Houses 1, 2, 3)

The first quadrant represents ME and MY MOM, and the physical body trying to develop, or formulate itself. The foundation of this world is devotion. In this stage, you are a dependent creature needing supplementation, and you need a source to be devoted to you.

This is where you formulate base beliefs about yourself, and the world around you. You perceive the environment through your emotions and feelings, which become the barometer indicating you have a need. How fast or slow, that devoted person responded to you creates your first perception of reality. At this stage, you believe your subjective reality is truth, and your physical experience as THE reality. You then create personalities based on your perception of the devotion you received.

As human beings, one of our problems is that we tend to see the world as linear – left and right, front and back, up and down. That is not reality – it is an illusion, a misperception. We build reality around our misperceptions, and they contain, organize and define our experiences. We believe the Sun goes up and down and around the Earth. We believe in light and dark, but that is a limited time and space perspective. If we could get far enough away from the Earth, we would see that light exists all the time. The first quadrant shows your subconscious philosophy, the tools you use to get needs met and the set up for your approach to life.

The First House is your underlying psychology and how you act for survival. Relationship model one symbolizes Aries. Your energy initiates to a source, seeking a response that is just for me. Feelings convert the responses into self-judgment, acceptance or rejection. This house shows your impulsive, compulsive drives.

- A crucial region to understand in astrology is the first house. In chart interpretation, the first house tells you the environment as an infant between you and your mother. It sets the context of how we as physical animals see reality. It shows you the drive that is pushing the body and how connected or disconnected, you are from the biological world.

- Known as your Rising Sign or Ascendant, it represents YOU. It is the internal you, the animal you, the emotional self and your relationship with Mom. Some people say it also represents your personality, but we have multiple personalities, so the whole chart represents many personalities.

- It describes your mother's approach to life at that time. The condition she was living, in relation to her family, her sense of placement in society, and the social arrangement or marriage she had with your father. This house indicates your mother's maturity level and ability to nurture and sacrifice for you as an infant, and how you interpreted her behavior.

- The first house is the infant experience. Since we are a dependent being at this stage, it also represents the "need to receive." The first three houses are fear based with the first house being the fear of not receiving. You then act to protect yourself, or seek to protect other people The tool structure of this house is emotions, demonstrated through crying, cooing, anger, smiles, touching, and eye contact. The Aries drive of the first house is cardinal, so it acts toward a source for security and protection.

- In the Aries phase of development, you are interpreting the source through your feelings, and the degree of agitation, or ease, in getting your needs met. You are learning what you must do to obtain security, which evolves into unconscious behavior that motivates how you act to resolve your personal needs.

The Second House is a stabilized self, who is independent of the source. Relationship model two symbolizes Taurus. You are seeking to stand on your own, but need supplementation from the source to assist in your completion, and respond "**to me.**" In the Taurus stage of life, you are independent of Mom one minute, but then need her. You want the freedom to explore, yet security to know you can go back to her. The tools of the second house are a sense of independence, the awareness of things around you, the ability to do for oneself and the need to possess.

- This house, ruled by Taurus and Venus, is a foundational identity, no matter how many other personalities you acquire through time. It represents the combination of attributes and abilities you innately possess, along with the tools the body brings into the world, what you have others can rely on, and basic values others experience. It shows how you will structure and support your family, what your expectation is from family, and your ability to sustain yourself, or rely on others. It also indicates your material assets, how you earn and handle monetary income, values and priorities you establish throughout life.

- This stage represents the principles and properties the physical body possesses, and the degree of confidence the body possesses. It shows if the body trusts providing for itself and how much it needs to rely on another person, situation, circumstance or the social order for a sense of its own value.

- The second house represents the interpretation of who you are in relationship with another, and your ability to trust that others will provide for you, and be someone to you. If you feel you cannot rely on others, then you may not conform or feel you can be part of the family.

The Third House is learning conformity and how to direct your energy for a benefit. Relationship model three symbolizes Gemini. At this stage, you are exploring and gathering information. You are beyond the Taurus' insecurity of abandonment and learning how to direct your energy towards what is beneficial. This is the "**about me"** phase, where you communicate about yourself, and want others to be about you and your interests.

- You use words and responses from others to gauge reality, and declare your likes and dislikes.
- You are beginning to conceptualize who people are and the hierarchal relationships that symbolically exist between them – mom, dad, brothers, sisters, aunts, uncles, grandparents—and calling them by name. At this point, you are learning to define the people and things in the environment that you can expect something from versus those you cannot, then directing energy towards those individuals with the expectation that they will direct their energy back.
- The family redirects your energy to conform to their beliefs, traditions, rituals and rules for acceptable and unacceptable behavior. You begin to attach concepts to people and things, such as "Good girl or good boy," "No!" "Don't do that." Your behavior is beginning to be modified through words and concepts, to conform to rules. This is where one may get punished for not conforming.
- As you learn to direct the body's energy towards things and people of benefit, this is a transition point between physical encounters and

psychological concepts. Physical restriction and various degrees of punishment direct the child and reinforce the views of the group. The amount of acceptance, or punishment at this stage, will make a significant difference in how we perceive belonging, or not belonging (which is the 4th house).

- Those who fail to develop in this phase will not advance their tool structures from physical gestures such as pouting, crying, withdraw, running away, anger, tantrums etc. They are still hoping someone will be aware of them and respond to these communicative tools. Despite the limitations it creates, this approach still becomes a more secure perspective.

- Those who are able to mature are evolving away from the body's reactions and responses, to interact through language and thought with other people. The third house indicates how well you can use words. This developmental stage is extremely powerful because you are beginning to get a reflection of yourself by the reaction of others—more than how they respond to you emotionally or physically. You may react to other's words and psychological pictures as being judgmental or saying something "about me." At this stage, you are using the mind as a tool to assess reality, versus just experiencing life and having feelings dictate your perceptions.

This last house of the first quadrant, ruled by Gemini, represents self expression, communication, one's mental state, the immediate environment or neighborhood, close relatives especially siblings, our elementary school experience and our early teachers.

The first quadrant should have no Water. Water represents emotional nurturing and devotion. In the first quadrant, there should not be Water because the Water we receive should be coming from the 12th House, which is the Pisces devotion from the mother. If you do have Water in the 1st, 2nd or 3rd House it means you believe you cannot regulate your mother, you have to bring the Water yourself. You have to bring devotion to yourself and give it to your mother, more than you were able to receive it from her. Cancer Water is bringing your own nurturing, or having to nurture your mother. Scorpio Water means you had to be committed to yourself and your mother. Pisces Water means, you had to be devoted to yourself and devoted to your mother, because she was unable to give that to you.

The Second Quadrant is the Southeast Portion of the Chart (Houses 4, 5, 6)

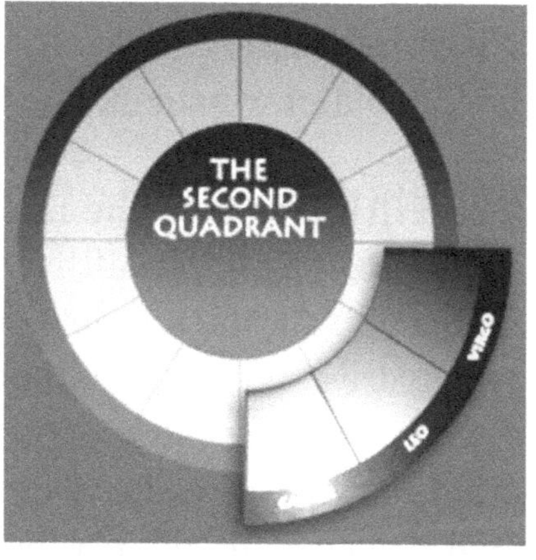

The second quadrant represents Me and My Family. This world is father-dominated to structure and solidify us as human beings. The hierarchy goes from having a sense of belonging from an emotional connection (Cancer), to being an individualized part of the group (Leo), and then responsible back to the family (Virgo). In this stage, you will often demonstrate by "doing things" for people in order to belong. If you have not mastered conforming you may get punished, ostracized, and feel separated from belonging.

The Fourth House drives the need to belong. Relationship model four symbolizes Cancer. It shows how your family approached raising children, your approach to family and society, the role that you play within the family, and what you must do to conform to the group and belong. You are now learning the roles, rules, approach and hierarchal relationship within the family, and the relationship of the group to the greater community. As you get older, and add your own friends and peer groups, you expand your lessons in group dynamics through involvement with community or educational organizations.

The same process of conformity within social groups, bases trust on the greater community taking your needs into consideration. If not, you may not conform to the larger community. This could create authority issues and antisocial behavior. Cancer and the fourth house are the "part of me" stage where you initiate to be cared for, and can care for others within the group. You are integrating others as part of yourself, presuming family and friends are interconnected. It also represents group judgment, acceptance or rejection, and the distress, which comes from believing you do not receive emotional caring.

This phase also initiates your trained identity. You are going to school and learning to put away your emotional identity for collective alignment. Characterized by discipline and obedience, you are learning compliance to time, following orders, to work independently and quietly. This identity can often find an outlet to achieve, beyond what you are experiencing at home.

The Fifth House is the need to individualize. Relationship model five symbolizes Leo. The fifth house defines your ego and who you are as a unique individual. You are an adolescent becoming aware of your own individuality and sexual drive. It is the first time that you seek to unite with another person, outside of your own security system, i.e. love, romance, sex, and pleasure, and want others outside of the family to be "with me." Within the family you are testing your independent identity, but are still dependent circumstantially on them.

- The fifth house Leo stage is puberty. It is projecting oneself as being unique, or different. Distress comes from not being able to get personal recognition. We want things to revolve around our specialness, but we may not be able to construct reality because we are still too young or immature, to move beyond the family, or home.
- The fifth house also represents speculation outside of your security needs, such as gambling or investments. The tools of the fifth house are individuality, ego, creative talent, pursuit of pleasure, romance, children and speculative ventures.

The Sixth House is responsibility driven. Relationship model six symbolizes Virgo. The last phase of the second quadrant is Virgo, where you are beginning to be in the energetic circle of giving and receiving. Up to this point, you focus on receiving energy. Virgo is the highest state in the physical world in which you learn responsibility back to those devoted to you. You act interdependent with the group, assisting, serving and playing roles, with both giving and receiving energy. You are able to represent the values of the group and know how to be "with you responsibly."

- The sixth house describes your role to family, especially the responsibilities you take on as an adult child. It also indicates how you must serve the spiritual well being of your family, including your biological family, your social family (through your job or career), and your collective family (the society at large).
- This house represents your employer and your approach to work – physical labor, daily tasks, those who work for or with you.
- It indicates your daily responsibilities, your ability to be a responsible person to others and sacrifice your ego identity, if necessary.
- It also represents your health and physical fitness, including attitudes about food and diet.
- The tools you use are: representing the group you came from, responsibility, practicality, perfectionism, analyzing and serving.
- There is a tendency to get consumed by the family – the family's needs and being someone responsible to the family. Distress comes from serving those who do give you recognition.

The second quadrant should have no Air. The element of Air represents ideas and agreements. In the second quadrant, you are to conform to the ideas and agreements of the family, not have your own thoughts and concepts away from the group. If you have Gemini in the 4th, 5th or 6th Houses, you are a nonconformist within family. If you have Libra in the second quadrant, you are choosing to belong with people outside of the family and make different choices than those in the family. If there is Aquarius in these houses you represent different beliefs, belong to a different social order, and are adding things to our life that are different from your family.

The Third Quadrant is the Northeast Portion of the Chart (Houses 7, 8, 9)

The Third Quadrant represents Me and My Relationships. You are now driven to merge and move beyond your biological family dictating reality and structuring your beliefs. The third quadrant represents relationship patterns that are merging with others beyond the original family. If you have considerable Libra, Scorpio or Sagittarius energy, you will notice that a lot of your language and processing comes through the lens of relationships and merging.

If you have mastered the previous phases, you bring responsibility skills to connect with another person. You are dissolving into a conceptual person, where motivations, actions and behaviors stem from being symbolic and conscious, more than physical. In an adult mature reality, you act by choice, merge through principles, stabilize through commitment and conform through beliefs.

The third quadrant is conscious. “I don’t need you. I desire to be with you and create with you, but I do not need you to exist.” In this phase, you are not just “with” someone. You are creating an agreement with another person about what constitutes reality. Together you have a concept about life that is driving your experiences. In order to do this, you must understand the perceptions and values of one another. You have to know how you both see reality, what is important and valued, and establish a perceptive agreement that you commit to align your behavior. Agreements then supersede physical perceptions, emotions and feelings.

The third quadrant is equivalent to the first quadrant in developing people. In the first quadrant, you are developing the physical, organic experience to prepare you to be in the family. The third quadrant is preparing you to be part of the collective family.

The Seventh House seeks relationships of choice and agreement. The 7th house, or Descendant, represents who we are as an independent person outside of the family. Once we move beyond parental influence, we start to define ourselves by our choices, relationships and partnerships.

Relationship model seven denotes Libra. We now have a compulsive need to be in a relationship, learning how to choose, and be in agreement with that which we choose or with that which chooses us. This is where we initiate actions toward another and fear possible rejection.

- The seventh house represents your approach to marriage, partnership, and joint ventures of any kind. It describes how you interact with people and how others tend to regard you.
- The seventh house corresponds with legal matters, negotiations, contracts and all open confrontations, pleasant or adversarial. The tools used are attractiveness, longing, likes, seduction, persuasion, and agreement. You are beginning to construct your relationships, not just from physical attraction, but from mutually constructing agreements with others.
- Distress occurs from disagreement about the nature and direction of the union.

The Eighth House is commitment driven. Relationship model eight exemplified by Scorpio is where you seek definition and commitment. You are moving beyond emotions and feelings as a basis of defining the relationship. You are interdependent and not meant to stand alone, so you stop battling for your own identity. Relationships are with each other through commitment.

- Desire to find completion with another person rules the eighth house and distress comes from not being able to define the commitment, or reeling from a lack of commitment. This may lead to power struggles and possession of the union for security but without having an agreement of what constitutes completion.

- This house represents the transformation of an individual's perception toward something or involvement in something. The tools used are resourcefulness, steadfastness, probing for deeper understanding, as well as secrecy, manipulation, power, persuasion, control and punishment.
- The eighth house relates to sexual attitudes and behavior, taxes, debt, death, legacies, inheritance and the income you receive through marriage or business partner(s).

The Ninth House is belief driven. Relationship model nine is the home of Sagittarius. The ninth house is a direct result of your encounters in the eighth. The key motivation is the desire for a definition to resolve relationship struggles. The tools you use are discipline, beliefs, integrity, principles, ideas, concepts and knowledge. It describes your beliefs about who you are in a relationship, and who you need to be based upon results from your relationships. You are now seeking belief systems to dictate the commitments that govern relationships. The hierarchy of directing energy is **with you in beliefs,** which means our agreements and beliefs supersede our physical perceptions, emotions and feelings. If we do not conform to belief systems, we run the risk of persecution.

- Your 9th House shows the beliefs you will approach life with, and the tools you will use to resolve issues in your life.
- It defines the information we use to guide our societies. It represents the development of the mind through higher education, advanced training, publishing, publicity, advertising, politics, foreign travel, foreign studies, religious and philosophical views and activities, and cultural pursuits. It defines relationships from a social perspective – love is law, not attraction.
- This house also represents the adult relationship you have with your family, and the battle over domination between society's religious and school structures versus the traditional tribal and family patterns. Many believe it also represents second marriage and in-laws.

If you can not adopt the principles of the third quadrant, you will flail around in the asteroid belt, attracted to people without responsibility or commitment, resembling broken down colliding matter with nothing solid to hold you together.

The third quadrant should have no Earth. The third quadrant has no Earth because you should merge with another person based on choice and agreement, commitment and beliefs. Earth is the ability to stand away from the source. If you have Taurus in the third quadrant, you believe you must be independent within the relationship. If you have Virgo in the 7th, 8th or 9th Houses, you may have an inability to separate from your family. Your partner may believe you are consumed by your original family's responsibilities and not fully committed to the relationship. If you have Capricorn in the third quadrant, your relationship is with your work first, and you feel you have to support yourself and others.

The Fourth Quadrant is the Northwest Portion of the Chart (Houses 10, 11, 12)

The energy of this quadrant is the Need to Create. The tools you use are creativity, cooperation, hard work, inventions, designing, management, structure and belief. When you reach the fourth quadrant, you are not operating as a "Me." You have matured to dissolve yourself into the collective, social purpose. You exist symbolically as a functioning role to something, becoming a component, facilitator and servant to the social and spiritual world.

The social world does not spawn emotionalism. It is an organized reality, which is obedience and discipline driven. You stabilize as an affiliated member through the concepts and philosophies of the collective. You conform as a devoted person to the well being of the group and uninitiated.

The Tenth House rules obligation and duty. Relationship model ten is Capricorn's natural home. This house shows what you approach with obligation and duty. It describes your ability to resolve the issues you had growing up, by creating your own reality, and stabilizing yourself as a socially responsible person. You create your placement to the greater family, which is the society itself.

- This house also reflects society's ability to recreate itself from the discoveries and new information that emanate from the ninth. These include scientific and technical discoveries and new devices. As we redefine our relationship to each other and the world around us, we gradually create our world to reflect the importance of these new decisions and relationships, i.e. affirmative action, women in the workplace. In other words, what we legislate redefines what we create to define our reality.
- The tenth house represents your father and his influence in your life, authority figures and your attitude towards authority.
- It is your career, professional goals, reputation, achievements, and honors. Ruled by Saturn, it also represents structure, societal laws, rules, and things that restrict us.

The Eleventh House is our social status and affiliation. Relationship model eleven is the energy of Aquarius. This is the idea world of Uranus, which is inclusive or exclusive, at times unusual, unexpected and bringing upheaval. It represents our social projection, associations, institutions, class affiliation, friendships and acquaintances, clubs, organizations, and humanitarian causes. Aquarius energy is **"with you in symbolic collective agreement"** for the creation of our cultural, social, political and economic reality.

- It is technology such as televisions, computers, the internet, and all ideas ahead of their time.

- The eleventh house represents the new things we add to our life. It rules friendships, membership organizations, and income derived from self-employment as opposed to wages earned from a job. This house represents the world where "we belong" and that of institutions as substitute family structures.
- This house is where one dissolves to represent collective agreement, and holds the motto of "I believe everyone belongs."
- The tools we use are institutions, organizations, social groupings, friendships, and any other detached form of bonding such as sororities, fraternities, gangs, teams, and politics. It relates to the role you play in the lives of others as a child, parent, lover, spouse, friend, social or business associate. It describes your hopes, aspirations, and plans for your future.

The Twelfth House is where you dissolve self to serve the well being of others through consciousness and devotion. **Relationship model twelve symbolized by Pisces,** is "**with you through tradition and service,"** devoted to advancing our beliefs and values. The twelfth house describes what you serve, and traditions passed down from previous generations. It represents what parents teach their children, e.g. beliefs, myths, laws, value, and approach to our life. To the young, this represents the hidden information you live by that controls the reality. This includes what you cannot see or understand beyond your mandatory roles to society. You only know the laws that will punish you for not playing these roles.

- The world of illusions and projection, this house shows the area you give devotion, the private and hidden side of life, the subconscious mind, dreams, and the past. It is that which is purposely deceptive, hidden enemies, suffering, guilt, repression or self doubt. On the higher side, it represents spiritual inspiration and intervention, enlightenment and sacrifice to others.

- Ruled by Neptune, this house shows your ability to project illusions that can appear to be real such as dreams, stories, movies, lies and deceits, alcohol, drugs, and any altered state of consciousness. It relates to sorrow, disappointment, loss, solitude or confinement, hidden fears and worry, as well as the job or health of your marriage or business partner. The twelfth house is the last stage where we all belong, and we serve who and what we belong to. The tools we use are contributing, sacrificing, serving, empathy, dissolving, masochism, loyalty, and devotion.

The fourth quadrant should have no Fire. Fire is the action principle, and in the fourth quadrant, you should not be acting on your own behalf. If you do have Fire in the fourth quadrant of the chart, you are bringing inappropriate actions. Aries in the fourth quadrant would mean you believe you must act on our own behalf. Leo means you require individual, social recognition and may be too self-involved. Sagittarius would indicate that you are trying to convert others to your beliefs, and may have too many separate beliefs than the collective.

Chapter Nine
Quadrant Exploration

Your Energetic Quadrant Profile

When you look at a chart, you can see what the dominant quadrant approach may be.

1. How many planets have a need to receive and are "self" focused?
   Number of Aries / Taurus / Gemini planets _______
   If you have four or more, you have a dominant first quadrant approach.

2. How many planets demand that you stand on your own?
   Number of Cancer / Leo / Virgo planets _______
   If you have four or more, you have a dominant second quadrant approach.

3. How many planets have a need to merge with another?
   Number of Libra / Scorpio / Sagittarius planets _______
   If you have four or more, you have a dominant third quadrant approach.

4. How many planets have a need to convert, give to others and exist as a symbolic social being?
   Number of Capricorn / Aquarius / Pisces planets _______
   If you have four or more, you have a dominant fourth quadrant approach.

Calculating the Degrees in Each Quadrant

Each house is normally 30 degrees, and since there are three houses per quadrant the total degrees would be 90. Each sign is also 30 degrees. You will find that the signs are usually split between two houses and not all degrees lie in each house.

How do you calculate this? If the rising sign is at 05 degrees of Cancer and then the second house starts at 26 degrees of Cancer, this means the total degrees of Cancer in the first house is 21 degrees (26-5). The second house then starts at 26 degrees of Cancer and goes to 20 degrees of Leo. Since there are 30 degrees per sign, and the second house starts at 26 degrees, there are only 4 degrees of Cancer left in this house (30 degrees minus 26 degrees). Then we add 20 degrees of Leo. The second house is a total of 4 degrees plus 20 which is 24 degrees. The third house starts at 20 degrees of Leo and goes to 18 degrees of Virgo. 30 degrees - 20 degrees, leaves 10 degrees of Leo left plus 18 degrees of Virgo. The third house is 10+18, or 28 degrees.

1st house = 21 degrees

2nd house = 24 degrees

3rd house = 28 degrees

The total for the first quadrant is 73 degrees.

If you are close to 90 degrees in your quadrants, then there is a more balanced approach to all worlds.

The first quadrant is the amount of time you get nurturing energy to formulate yourself.

Less than 90 degrees conclude quickly, basing reactions on fear, and formulating conclusions without exploring in any depth. You try to formulate without having enough internal stuff as a self to be able to complete or conform. It is like you are baking a cake that has to be in the oven for an hour and a half and it comes out in 45 minutes. You put the toothpick into the cake, and it is gooey. You cut the cake, and it falls apart. You can not formulate into a person prepared to feel part of the family (which is the second quadrant).

Anyone who did not have 90 degrees is still seeking devotion as a primary drive. You look to be in a relationship with somebody dedicated to you. If the first quadrant is short, then the second quadrant is essential because you need the support of the people in your family to solidify you. You would not have the true internal skills to trust yourself.

If you have more than 90 degrees, you keep taking in a lot of information before you formulate yourself. You spend extra time putting things together. It is like being in the computer industry, and once one model comes out there is an updated version already in the planning stage. Ideas keep evolving.

When you have the rising signs of Sagittarius, Capricorn, Aquarius, and Pisces in the first quadrant there is usually more than 90 degrees. It takes longer to formulate your identity.

The second quadrant is the amount of time you get energy in the family world to solidify yourself. If you have less than 90 degrees, then you do not spend much time in the family world solidifying self. If you have more than 90 degrees, there is an over emphasis on family as you solidify, whether it is conscious or subconscious dependency, or responsibility to family. It also indicates that you put a lot of energy into becoming a solid person, often through an emphasis on schooling and classes.

The third quadrant is where you merge with another in union. *(Note: The number of degrees in the first quadrant will be the same in the third quadrant.)*

If you have less than 90 degrees in the third quadrant of relationships, you also have less than 90 degrees in the first quadrant. Since you did not have enough devotion to developing an internal sense of trust, you would have a hard time brining a complete trusting person into relationships.

If you have more than 90 degrees, then the bulk of your experiences in life revolve around yourself and your relationships. You are spending a lot of time formulating yourself and merging in unions.

The fourth quadrant is where you dissolve self into a symbolic projection of a belief serving the collective. *(Note: The number of degrees in the second quadrant will be the same in the fourth quadrant.)*

If you have less than 90 degrees, in the fourth quadrant it means you did not get your solidity from the family, or work. If you have more than 90 degrees, then family experiences and your external identity have a major emphasis. You will have a lot of focus on group interactions.

How to Interpret Quadrant Placements in the Chart

If you have done any chart interpretation, you realize that most often the signs that occupy the houses do not follow the natural flow of starting with Aries in the first house, and ending with Pisces in the 12th house. So here is a simplified guide to a quadrant approach to interpretation.

The signs in your first quadrant (Houses 1, 2, 3) show the relationship with your mother.

Aries / Taurus / Gemini in the first quadrant indicate that you are physically reactive and responsive to stimuli. As you mature through different stages, you must control your emotions and fears, and stabilize your independence to direct your energy away from the source, who in most cases is your mother. You don't trust being dependent because you had to fortify yourself as a child and fortify your mother.

Cancer / Leo / Virgo in Houses 1, 2, 3 indicate that in your formulating years family played a dominant role in conditioning you. You are examining your ability to solidify yourself within the group by being cared for and part of the group (Cancer rising), by exploring your individuality and uniqueness as a member of the group (Leo rising), or by taking on responsibility within the group (Virgo rising). You will also assist others in their ability to solidify through groups. If you have Cancer in the first quadrant, you believe you had to nurture yourself.

Libra / Scorpio / Sagittarius in Houses 1, 2, 3 indicate you had to be in a relationship and merge with your mother. From childhood through adult relationship, you must give of yourself before you can receive. You come into the world with the ability to be responsible and committed to whatever is devoted to you. If you have Scorpio in the first quadrant, you have to be committed to yourself. Third quadrant signs are directing energy beyond the group and seeing life in terms of relationships.

Capricorn / Aquarius / Pisces in Houses 1, 2, 3 indicates an individual older than their years, who learns early on to dissolve or submerge their needs, and creates an identity that plays roles to the mother or others. You are formulated by the external world, and find yourself by merging with the greater society. You tend to act towards the world with devotion. If you have Pisces in the first quadrant, you have to be devoted to yourself. With this dynamic, you may carry unresolved emotional deficits because you were not seen as having to be catered to emotionally.

The signs in your second quadrant (Houses 4, 5, 6) indicate the world that solidifies you.

Aries / Taurus / Gemini mean you were independent, self-protective and a non-conformist within the family. You felt you had to solidify yourself. If Gemini shows up in the second quadrant, it means you cannot conform to the family.

Cancer / Leo / Virgo in Houses 4, 5, 6 is the natural energy for these houses and indicates that you seek to solidify and stabilize yourself within the family. There is also a tendency to find a sense of belonging with other families outside of your own.

Libra / Scorpio / Sagittarius in the second quadrant indicate that relationships are what solidify you. If you have Libra in the second quadrant, you make choices differently than the family, or do not agree with their choices.

Capricorn / Aquarius / Pisces in the second quadrant, indicates that you found a sense of belonging and solidity within the collective environment of schools, associations, institutions and/or religions. Aquarius in the second quadrant means you have different social ideas than the family.

The signs in your third quadrant show your approach to relationships.

Aries / Taurus / Gemini in the third quadrant Houses 7,8,9 indicates a person who does not trust receiving, and operates independently in relationships, in a self-protective and a nonconformist way. If you have Taurus in the third quadrant, you may separate from relationships because of your mother.

Cancer / Leo / Virgo in Houses 7,8,9 indicates a person who is overly committed to their original family. They treat relationships more like friends and peer groups. If there is Virgo in the third quadrant, you may separate from your relationships because of your family responsibilities.

Libra / Scorpio / Sagittarius in houses 7,8,9 usually indicates a person often in relationship with people who are in relationship with someone else. There may also be a number of incomplete relationships in the search for commitment and a shared belief.

Capricorn / Aquarius / Pisces in houses 7,8.9 indicates a person who often prioritizes their career, their social identity or devotion to a cause outside of the relationship. They are mainly in relationship with the collective and external social world. If there is Capricorn in the third quadrant, you may separate from the relationship because of work.

The signs in your fourth quadrant show your approach to the social world.

Aries / Taurus / Gemini in the fourth quadrant indicates a person whose career and social identity are their personal reflection. The individual's personal issues may interfere, and they may need to develop maturity when interacting socially. If you have Aries Fire in the fourth quadrant, you act for your own self-survival, not necessarily for the group.

Cancer / Leo / Virgo in the fourth quadrant indicate a person who seeks to belong socially. They will need to receive some ego recognition for what they do and/or the responsibility skills they bring. If you have Leo in the fourth quadrant, you act for social recognition.

Libra / Scorpio / Sagittarius in Houses 10, 11, 12 indicate a person who can bring agreements, commitment and beliefs into their social interactions and positions. If you have Sagittarius in the fourth quadrant, you act to convert others to your beliefs.

Capricorn / Aquarius / Pisces in Houses 10, 11 12 is a natural placement. It indicates a person who is often more comfortable socially than personally, and able to be socially responsible, obligated and devoted.

Chapter Ten
Cosmic DNA Spotlights

Some astrologers confuse their clients with astrological nomenclature and mystifying rhetoric. My intention is to provide straightforward approaches to a complex subject matter and interpretive tools to see energetic patterns in a chart, the subconscious drives and motivations, strengths and challenges. Everyone who does chart interpretation knows there are multiple layers to the evaluation. Along with the energetic profile, spotlighting your Cosmic DNA is an expedient place to begin organizing one's interpretation of a chart.

Let's start with features, of your Cosmic DNA, to assist in assimilating the various layers used to perceive and approach life. When looking at a solar map, the first thing we assess is how the organic self is conditioned and structured. Then we assess the belief systems one uses to contain, organize and define the world. The following components of one's solar map assist us in this exploration.

Your Sun Sign

Your sun sign shows you the developmental stage your soul has evolved to, and the center from where it operates. It represents the level of consciousness and evolvement you come into the world with, the technologies you personally use to confront and address the situations around your birth, and the circumstances you encounter.

Each Sun sign is an archetype that represents a consistent pattern of emotional, physical, and symbolic perspectives, with distinct approaches. Based on your archetype, we can define the approach you will use to perceive, symbolize, synthesize, and regulate your relationship to the environment. It also indicates the roles you play to others, the people who come to bask in your light, whether you are the Equatorial Sun, the Arctic Sun or someplace with variable heat and light. Your Sun's placement in your map will reveal the people and circumstances that will seek your energetic rays. Remember, the Sun represents our identity and individuality, ego, main direction and focus, as well as our core personality approach to life. (See chapter 5 for the personality traits of the different signs.)

The Rising Sign

Your rising sign indicates the psychological situation you were born into, and the conditioning that sets up how you were formulated in the first one to two years of life. This includes the mother/child relationship and bonding experience, maturity level of the parents, and the tools you learned to pacify the body and receive from that initial environment. (See chapter 7 for descriptions of the rising signs.)

The Moon Sign

The Moon sign determines how one measures emotional time and space. As children, one experiences the relationship with Mom through the emotions. This relationship becomes the myth one constructs about self and the mother. This is crucial because the condition of the moon's environment determines the length of time it takes between your emotional desire and the gestation period for that desire to be satisfied. Each relationship model will address and respond to emotional cues differently. *Note: When you are analyzing a child's astrology chart, the moon is crucial to understand because the child's emotional self evolves more rapidly than one's Sun sign identity.*

Moon in Aries - are emotionally reactive if not responded to immediately. Believe they must protect themselves emotionally at all times.

Moon in Taurus - as an Earth sign will try to stabilize themselves during sensitive times and fears emotional abandonment. Love companionship and do not like emotional outbursts.

Moon in Gemini - like the Air signs Libra and Aquarius, are more analytical about their feelings, and yours. They need to talk about their thoughts and feelings, and are happy to help others "talk through their problems." They are restless and get bored very easily.

Moon in Cancer - like all Water signs feel emotions more deeply than Fire, Earth or Air signs. The Moon in Cancer is in its home placement, which will emotionally nurture and relate to the feelings of others, but feels no one relates to them.

Moon in Leo - this fire sign needs emotional recognition and reassurance that they are "special". Very loyal partners, this placement needs a lot of love (more than they will tell you) and their sense of pride when hurt may act out.

Moon in Virgo - feels emotionally responsible for their mother and must represent her. Many with this placement absorbed criticism from their mother as children and have low self- esteem. They get stressed, like routines, keep their feelings to themselves and want to be needed by others.

Moon in Libra - placement loves companionship – they do not like to be alone and they do not hide their feelings very well. They need to have their way, and may continue to debate their point until they win. They do not like aggression or violence. Their moods may fluctuate, and they can be indecisive, but they are usually charming and cheerful about it.

Moon in Scorpio - feels emotionally deprived of the mother's love during some point in life. Go into bouts of emotional isolation, so they need commitment. They are intuitive, creative and adept at understanding others on a deeper level. They may be suspicious, possessive and secretive until they feel secure, then they are loyal and protective.

Moon in Sagittarius - have enthusiastic personalities, but if there is a problem they often disappear before working through issues. They need experiences, independence and freedom while being spontaneous, impatient, competitive and candid.

Moon in Capricorn - are serious, ambitious and may appear cold are traits often used to describe Capricorn Moon individuals. They do not like to expose their feelings. Displays of affection may not be second nature because they didn't pick that up when they were young. They need respect and will take on responsibility whether at home or work. Because they hold on to anger and resentment, it can lead to illness or depression as well as explosions once they hit their limit of holding back their feelings.

Moon in Aquarius - are emotional observers who analyze others and have a more detached manner with people. There is a strong need for independence. They do not like clingy and insecure people. Mostly out of touch with their own emotions, they do not like criticism. They prefer to stay in the realm of intellect, intuition and creativity.

Moon in Pisces - possess sensitivity, empathy and caring, which predisposes them to be devoted to their mother's condition in life, as well as other people. They are romantic, intuitive and even psychic. Often preferring to live in the dream world, many are actors, writers, musicians or artists. The ability to relate to others can turn into becoming overly involved, drained, and manipulated.

Saturn Measures Reality

We all start out as an organic being and physical creature. As we develop, the body becomes a vehicle converted to represent something beyond just an organic form. Look at the State of California. Like the rest of the United States, it is just land. There is no such thing as California, except as a construct with artificially generated boundaries, definitions and laws. That is the energy of Saturn. Each planet represents a principle that overlays reality. It organizes, contains and restricts reality to rules, roles and laws. Saturn's energy is law, government, corporations and the political process. Saturn is measurement, structure and definition of time and space.

Saturn's placement (sign and house) indicates how you organize your life, what structures you and the hierarchal personality people will meet on a continual basis. Saturn represents obsessive and compulsive drives, how you will approach your obligations, the law that governs you as a person and psychological restrictions you must conquer.

Saturn will compartmentalize life into grids. Let's look at a house. Saturn divides the space into separate rooms. There is a kitchen, living room, bathroom, bedrooms etc. The grids keep distinct energy separate. You don't take the kitchen and put the bathroom in that space. Saturn is how you divide and organize your life by principles.

Saturn in Aries - divide things into different compulsions. There is a compulsive need to act for oneself, and organize life around self, starting and formulating an identity. There is a need to be you, but that is where one gets restricted or punished. There may be selfishness until one learns how to trust others and/or help those who are also trying to formulate an identity. The body is still young and reactive as it seeks to get its needs met.

Saturn in Taurus - locks one into long-term responsibilities. They are compulsively trying to find their own sense of value, purpose and security. Taurus means one stands away from things, so everything stands away from everything else. They are independent over here and independent over there. Each room is independent of the other – they do not even touch each other. This placement can be irrational because they do not understand how to merge with others, so they often isolate themselves.

Saturn in Gemini - is difficult because Saturn wants to structure and Gemini wants to explore and be a nonconformist. They have many opinions, likes and dislikes, and do not want to be told how to do something. There is a tendency to go in different directions and direct their energy to people and things that are not of benefit.

Saturn in Cancer - has an obsessive and compulsive drive to understand the nature of home and group belonging. They do not feel a sense of belonging or fitting in with groups. They will strive to make others feel they belong, or become adamant about people they don't feel should be part of the group.

Saturn in Leo - has a need to pursue their own identity, and structure life around themselves. There may be an overemphasis on one's sexuality as a way of regenerating self and finding a greater sense of individuality through that vehicle.

Saturn in Virgo - represents responsibility and service. Saturn in Virgo cannot escape being responsible to the family. They must represent the behavior of the group, and play roles to maintain the group's solidity. Responsibilities organize their life.

Saturn in Libra - demonstrates an obsessive need to be in a relationship, but there may wind up having issues with their partners. They struggle with making the right choices.

Saturn in Scorpio - experiences a lack of commitment from males, and this deprivation of male energy contributes to a sense of deprivation. Their obsessive and compulsive drive is to make choices or commitments to ways that they have not fully chosen, or experience the inability to be committed to their choice.

Saturn in Sagittarius - is an obsessive, compulsive drive to convert yourself, or other people to a belief system, and that determines reality more than feelings. There is a tendency to be argumentative because conversations are an opportunity to convert people to their way of thinking.

Saturn in Capricorn - is in its natural placement. Here, one has a compulsive need to work, and it often denotes a lot of money. Mature people with this energy convert themselves into an obligated person who brings organization, structure and responsibility skills. There may be an obsession with achievement and recognition.

Saturn in Aquarius - compulsively combines things that do not necessarily go together. They organize themselves by their social status or social groupings. They also have ideas about how society should work, and compulsively seek to add their perspectives. This may create issues for them because their ideas are not main stream. They are usually ahead of their time, and idealistic.

Saturn in Pisces - has a compulsive need to be devoted, but actions towards others wind up denying them or turning them into a martyr. They may suffer from a lot of illusions, delusions, or subconscious views that are defeating, which does not help their susceptibility to addictions.

Our Cosmic DNA also gives a window to look into our evolutionary confrontations. As long as you have the time of birth, to see the house placements of the planets and signs, it will show the house that Scorpio is ruling in your chart, and where Pluto resides. Scorpio and Pluto energy represent personal confrontations, strains and areas of challenge in this lifetime. These become our metamorphosis callings.

Where Scorpio Sits in Your Chart You Discombobulate and Seek Commitment

Scorpio's placement in your solar map represents Plutonic energy residing in the asteroid belt. This is where matter breaks down into particles and chunks, and it is difficult to maintain consistency without a conscious commitment. Your Scorpio placement becomes a point of challenge, where you seek to be a solid and stable individual, beyond the internal voices that are constantly destabilizing your perceptions. Scorpio energy has the power and strength to transform these areas as long as you force yourself to get to the other side. You must stop allowing your incomplete internal needs to determine the nature of how you deal with yourself and other people. To evolve, you must learn to rise above the discontentment through definition and beliefs.

Scorpio in the 1st House means that your identity cannot maintain itself and you seek people to be committed to you. Your emotional overwhelm will kick you out of your own desire.

Scorpio in the 2nd House challenges the degree of confidence the body has to maintain self- reliance and resources.

Scorpio in the 3rd House means you have a tendency to break down when it comes to directing your own energy. Different environments may discombobulate you, more than you are grounded into who you are regardless of the situations you encounter.

Scorpio in the 4th House indicates that your family dynamics become a personal challenge. You feel deprived of a sense of belonging in family.

Scorpio in the 5th House indicates that you can't maintain your individuality within your family. You may even discombobulate when it comes to your sexual identity. You seek people to be committed to your individualization.

Scorpio in the 6th House means your break down when it comes to serving people. You probably had to serve your mother at a particularly early age, and responsibilities within the family are a source of deprivation.

Scorpio in the 7th House means you must transform how you make choices in relationships and partnerships.

Scorpio in the 8th House means that you feel deprived of commitment within your unions.

Scorpio in the 9th House challenges how you think and believe. You must transform your belief systems.

Scorpio in the 10th House indicates one who feels deprived in their jobs, and has to stabilize into a socially responsible person.

Scorpio in the 11th House means that you become destabilized in group associations and affiliations, institutions and social groupings.

Scorpio in the 12th House denotes that you will fall apart when it comes to tradition and what you must serve. It challenges you to transform the subconscious aspects of yourself.

Pluto Represents Your Life Drive

Each of us has a place where we struggle, where we are blocked from fulfillment and bliss, peace and contentment. Wherever Pluto sits in your chart is where you meet your evolutionary confrontation. Pluto's placement in your astrological chart represents your life drive, or the unconscious parameter that you struggle to go beyond to find completion. There is a demand to evolve beyond using the body, feelings, or emotions to dictate, assess or create reality in this area of life. You must use thought and consciousness.

Pluto in 1st House - blocks the path to your identity. You cannot formulate your identity as if you are always invisible. You cannot get enough information from others to get a self-reflection.

Pluto in the 2nd House - is the house of self-love and stability. Pluto destroys your ability to have a sense of your value and solidifying your identity. You must overcome, not loving yourself.

Pluto in the 3rd House - the house of Gemini, challenges your ability to direct your energy, to those within the environment who will be of benefit. Pluto limits the ability to conform, or have conscious agreements in your exploration. When Pluto sits here, either you, or others, don't live up to your agreements, and you may experience long term sibling conflicts. You must learn the nature of agreements and to cooperate and conform to the rules of environments where you seek to belong.

Pluto in the 4th House - the house of Cancer represents the death of you by trying to receive security and recognition from the family. Depending upon the sign Pluto is in, trying to actualize that principle, will often emotionally and psychologically prevent you from maturing. You present an identity that appears you belong, but that is not how you feel, and you will have a lot of family frustrations.

Pluto in the 5th House - blocks your ability to individualize and represents projecting identities that you have not yet actualized. Issues may develop once you reach puberty. Even though, your body is maturing, you will psychologically operate immaturely. You will have a need to individualize away from the group but always be psychologically connected to them.

Pluto in the 6th House - represents the death of you trying to break free of the family's expectations. The more you try, the more you die. The family expects you to serve them, but doing so represents your death and denies you the ability to have a choice. You artificially create an identity to interface with people and present a responsible character, but are irresponsible to your own well-being.

Pluto in the 7th House - represents the inability to choose and merge consciously. The world of relationships will be a continual enigma. It also means you won't make choices similar to your family. You won't merge with their process, or their way of life. You will merge with other groupings. You will also project merging with a false identity that is not totally involved in the relationship.

Pluto in the 8th House - means you can't be in union with the group you came from, and commitments elude you. There is an inability to merge with people based on physical or emotional reference points. You are often in union with other people's needs, more than committed to the person.

Pluto in the 9th House - means societal constructs or belief systems do not work for you. You must pursue your own truth because you could not rely on the belief systems that the family used to support and supply you. You will have different perceptions and beliefs about how to live life. This may create a lot of separation and confusion because your relationships would be dramatically different from the perception of what relationships should be, according to your beliefs about relationships.

Pluto in the 10th House - will isolate you socially. It will initially allow you to plug into the educational model, or the social work model, but it will eventually remove you from actualizing in that world. You will be seeking a social identity when you may not be able to find a family identity. You will constantly find yourself in some form of struggle until you learn to rely on and include the beliefs and structure of others.

Pluto in the 11th House - is the world of inclusion and exclusion. Social groups will either include you, or exclude you, and you are always trying to fit into a social order. You may be prevented from knowing how to fit in, and be accepted by various groups and organizations. You project yourself as fitting in, but you are often an outcast and misfit.

Pluto in the 12th House - is sitting in the hidden areas of life and the unconscious. Your evolution relies on not letting subconscious drives rule. Your mother had many perceptions about the concept of devotion, but you did not get the biological devotion necessary from her, and you repeat this in subsequent relationships. You must stop seeking this energy from others and learn to be devoted and dedicated to yourself.

Where Pluto sits in your chart, you artificially present a personality that is not your true identity. It is a personality you may or may not relate to but you present that personality so you can live within the construct of that environment. What you may not realize are the health issues associated with your life drive, and how they are inhibiting participation in certain areas of your life. They are creating discomfort through misperceptions and misfiring emotions that trigger your nervous system, causing you to experience stress, anxiety, depression, fear, anger and confusion.

Now what? The only path that remains once Pluto has touched an area of your life is consciousness. Pluto does not destroy the potential it destroys the organic involvement in it. You cannot use your body, feelings, or emotions to dictate, assess, or create reality. You must use thought and consciousness.

Understanding your Cosmic DNA is the process of embracing the multiple energetic components that reveal themselves in various motivations and personality traits. As an astrologer, the joy is helping people understand who they are beyond their Sun sign, how one is energetically predisposed to approach life, the cycles they are going through, and based on awareness, how to elevate their strengths and challenges into a conscious approach towards one's goals in life.

www.ingramcontent.com/pod-product-compliance
Lightning Source LLC
LaVergne TN
LVHW081320110826
845149LV00006B/1549